Organize Your Life!

Organize Your Life!

Skills you need to conquer the areas of chaos in your life.

Gretchen W. Cook

BELLA LUNA
PRODUCTIONS

Organize Your Life! The skills you need to conquer the areas of chaos in your life.
Copyright © 2006 by Gretchen W. Cook. Manufactured in the United States of America.
All rights reserved. No part of this book may be reproduced in any form or by any elec-
tronic or mechanical means including information storage and retrieval systems without
advance, written permission from the publisher, except by a reviewer, who may quote brief
passages in a review. Published by Bella Luna Productions, LLC, 2727 Old Canton Road,
Suite 294, Jackson, MS, 39216. (P.O. Box 4406, Jackson, MS 39296)
601-366-0901; 1-877-466-7927

First Edition.

ISBN: 0-9767013-0-8
Library of Congress Control Number: 2005910585

Designed by Caroline Kimbrough
Cover design by Cindy Clark

To Bill.
Thanks for your incredible
encouragement and support.

Contents

Introduction: Why Are We So Disorganized?

In today's society there are a number of warring cultural forces. When we find ourselves bombarded by too many lifestyle choices, many of which are equally valid (and some definitely not), we have much greater difficulty making the decisions and priority choices we need to live more organized lives. For example, when faced with an excess of food—say, a buffet—humans eat to excess. This principle may also apply to areas beyond food.

Overabundance

One of the most compelling societal factors is our time of relative prosperity. We live in a world of abundance. As a culture we are faced with a bewildering array of choices. There are too many options and too much stuff out there to not lead to confusion. Most towns have strips of fast food outlets along commercial arteries. Thus driving along one of those packed stretches becomes not a question of "Am I hungry?" but rather one of, "What am I hungry for?" Add in a passenger and your car can become paralyzed by indecision. Tacos? Hamburgers? Shakes? In the retail outlet the same thing can happen. Do you want the black pants, the navy blue pants? Why not both?

While abundance is obvious when discussing material possessions, it is also a problem when considering non-material choices as well. It is Friday. That means a night of entertainment. Do you choose cable television, a movie, a rental video? What about the play opening at the Little Theatre? Then there are the season tickets to the symphony you splurged for in a fit of cultural sophistication.

By the weekend you've had to make hundreds of choices about how to spend your time and money. If you have kids, Saturday will be another marathon of excess: soccer, children's birthday parties, a swim meet, and a trip to the Discount Mega Mart for school supplies for a project due Monday. This pace doesn't even leave room for household activities that accumulate undone, for weeks, until the holiday season hits like a hurricane. Whew.

Abundance is not bad in and of itself. But when over-abundance adds to your chaos instead of helping to address it, abundance can be considered a negative force in your life.

Here is one last note about an abundance of choices. Research has shown that when there are a lot of choices, sometimes the decision maker ends up paralyzed. For example, the more options in a retirement plan, the lower the employee participation. Overabundance can lead to chaos when the abundance causes delays in decision-making.

> When over-abundance adds to your chaos instead of helping to address it, abundance can be considered a negative force in your life.

Self-Indulgence

Another trend in our culture that leads to disorganization is the self-indulgence we have fostered as a society. We've been told, "You deserve it," when faced with a choice—usually requiring the sacrifice of our money. Luxurious bed linens, entire chain stores of wonderfully scented bath oils and soaps, empowerment workshops…a bustling industry operates on the premise that you deserve good things, and that no one will give them to you unless you do.

Self-indulgence is not intrinsically a bad thing, but when it develops into habits that lead to disorganization, it becomes a burden to your life, not a soothing, relaxing entitlement. You do deserve good things, but not at the peril of your checkbook, your household order or your mental well being.

Frugality

The frugality movement is a trend that operates in apparent opposition to the self-indulgence school of thought. And yet frugality, as described by many newsletters and books, is anything but simple. One amusing example of frugality I once read about was saving those plastic six-pack rings. Did you know that if you save enough of those things, you could make your own volleyball net? While I believe recycling is admirable, I also want to be able to reside in my home. Unless I happen to be living in a four-acre warehouse, I am not sure my top priority will be to collect six-pack rings until I have enough to make a volleyball net.

Another almost silly example I found on a web site was this: A woman with back problems was required to take several hot showers each day to help ease her pain. Because so much water was wasted while waiting for the shower water to get hot, she boasted that she collected it in jugs to water her plants. I wonder if her back problems aren't from lugging all that water around!

If you are organized, many elements of the frugality movement will be extremely useful. And if savvy frugality can allow you to quit your day job, maybe you'll have time to keep up with your six-pack rings. Frugality can be a good thing—but if it causes you to become a pack rat, re-evaluate. Very few pack rats live serene lives.

You do deserve good things, but not at the peril of your checkbook, your household order or your mental well being.

Simplicity Movement

Legions of folks have 'opted out' and voluntarily downsized themselves into a way of life that they believe is easier, more pleasant and therefore more rewarding than the oft-praised power career track. Some of the most fervent endorsements of this lifestyle come from the very people who occupied the power career track and were extremely successful at it.

The simplicity movement has in it elements of frugality is well as elements of self-indulgence. But in many ways simplicity is not all that simple. It involves making many decisions, and becoming skilled at making the decisions that result in a paring-down of excess in life.

To maintain a "simple" lifestyle, you must be ardent in the thinking and prioritizing skills that were used to downsize the life. The choice of a simple life is not a one-time decision, but rather a series of choices that must be upheld and reinforced by later choices, or the result will be a new lifestyle that is just as hectic and complex as the previous version—just in a different way. You may altruistically retire early to do important volunteer work in your life, only to find your Day Timer® packed with new obligations that drain just as much energy as your old schedule.

> The choice of a simple life is not a one-time decision, but rather a series of choices that must be upheld and reinforced by later choices, or the result will be a new lifestyle that is just as hectic and complex as the previous version.

Multi-Tasking Humans

This century yields opportunity for human beings as never before. Futurists predict the average worker will have seven careers during his or her work life. Not seven jobs, but seven careers. Now add to this the non-work roles everyone assumes, such as spouse, parent, care-taking child, volunteer, coach, housekeeper, chauffeur, and counselor. If you consider that for at least some of these career changes, new skills will require stints in higher education and/or vocational training, you'll have to add "life-long student" to the list of roles. This prospect implies a life of tremendous change and stress, peaking at various points around career switches and geographic moves.

Lifestyle upheaval is not only very stressful, but also very chaotic, even during the most well-organized transition. Given that at least some of these transitions will be involuntary, (i.e., caused by corporate downsizing, divorce, death, or natural disaster) the modern lifestyle, at least as envisioned by the early 21st century imagination, appears to be as challenging as the agrarian culture that suffered drought, floods and invasions in medieval Europe.

TV Peer Pressure

Do you think peer pressure only comes from your peers? Think again. Marketers rely on the ease with which they can sway American opinions and desires. Television is a huge transmitter of discontentment. It used to be that TV shows induced envy because we were so tempted to compare our average lives to the make-believe lives we peeked into.

It is actually worse today, because we've gotten into a steady diet of home shows, cooking shows and gardening shows. Now we don't just peek into impossible-to-really-live lives and homes, we get detailed "how to" instructions on creating the illusion for ourselves in our own lives. So now, rather than just a sneaking suspicion, we know our lives are deficient.

The Result

These influences (and there are many more I could describe) pull us in many different directions at once, leaving us stressed out and tired. When we are under strain and tired, organization is one of the first things to fly out the window.

We're exhausted, so we leave a few things undone in the office as we leave for the day. We're tired when we get home, and so some of the chores we thought we might tackle get left undone. We go to bed late, because apathy left us watching the late news, even though we didn't care and are so stressed out by tomorrow's meeting that we can hardly cope with one more smiling newscaster telling us the latest crime statistic.

Still tired, we get up late the next morning, only to discover the undone chores included laundering the shirt we wanted to wear this morning. Leaving the house late, there's just no time for breakfast. The drive-in line wasn't that long, so we risked it and turned into the restaurant parking lot.

We arrive at work breathless, a few minutes late, with biscuit crumbs in the creases of our clothes, only to discover the work fairy didn't complete the items left undone last night. The meeting is in ten minutes, and it looks like this is the best part of what will only be a hectic, maddening day.

When you live like this, you are not in control—chaos is.

How This Book Will Help
The intent of this book is not to tell you which of the many lifestyle options out there to choose. It is not to tell you what choices to make in the many decisions you are faced with each day. Rather, this book will help you develop thinking skills that will foster self-organization. If you want specific advice on precisely how to organize a closet, this book will only be marginally helpful. If you are hoping to learn how to think about your clothes, your wardrobe and your closet in a way that will help you first organize this area of your life and then maintain the system you develop, this book is for you.

By focusing on thinking skills, this book will allow you to adapt an organization style that will fit your lifestyle, whether it is one of luxurious self-indulgence or Spartan-like simplicity. Hopefully your life will yield fulfilling characteristics of both: simplicity in areas where simplicity fosters your creative energies, and decadent luxury in areas when your life needs a little TLC.

The Ten Principles
The thinking skills we will develop are based on ten principles of organization that will be first described, and then applied to some of the most common organizational challenges most people face. Much like taking a piece of cut crystal and turning it in your hands, these principles will be applied differently in different facets of everyday

life. These facets, as in crystal, can be viewed multiple ways. For our purposes, we will look at "organizational thinking" as it applies to material objects, your social arena, your work and your home.

Self Discipline and Organization

As one popular self-help speaker has said, "Everyone has the same amount of self-control. It is 100%!" Significant improvement in organizational skills is possible for everyone who is willing to change some behaviors, thinking patterns and actions. This book calls for change, and the most helpful types of personal change are almost always internally driven.

Discipline can mean rules, and consequences for breaking those rules. But a better definition for our purposes might be this: Discipline is a practice that leads to your getting what you want out of life.

Think about it. In the areas where you need to have discipline to be successful, you are nearly always in pursuit of getting something better out of your life for yourself. Discipline in exercise? You'll live longer and healthier. Discipline in finances? You'll have the economic resources to do what you want with your money, instead of having your paycheck absorbed by paying for items you used up months ago.

Discipline in organization doesn't mean mindless adherence to strict, fun-robbing rules. Instead, it means expending the time and energy to conquer areas of chaos in your life, thereby freeing your energy to devote to other, more rewarding aspects of your life. When you are more organized, life is easier. When life is easier, you have more fun.

> "Everyone has the same amount of self-control. It is 100%!"

Let the fun begin!

1

Basic Organization Skills

"Organized is not a destination, but a journey."
— Barbara Hemphill

Before we begin, there are some things you need to know about organization.

Clutter is the enemy of organization.

■ Clutter is the biggest enemy of organization. In our wealthy society, we simply suffer from too many options in too many instances. In this book I will talk about overabundance and how to cure it. Clutter goes beyond too many knick-knacks in the living room. It can include an overscheduled calendar, negative friendships that rob you of energy, and old commitments that no longer fit your life. With the help of this book we will eliminate clutter in our houses and our lives.

■ An organized life is organized internally as well as externally. The tidiest closet in the world is of no use if its owner is in inner turmoil from disorganized thinking. The best laid out workspace is useless if you really hate your job. Clearer thinking is often associated with goal setting. Goal setting is linked to knowing what you want out of life. It is hoped that as you begin to organize your life, you'll spend some time thinking about your internal life: what you hope to get out of this book and your life.

■ Organization is ongoing. Just like housework, it has to be done regularly and at frequent intervals. The good news is that you can develop your own system so that being organized becomes a rewarding habit.

■ Organization is 95% making decisions. Chaos is the result of postponed decision making. If you will hone your decision-making skills as you read this book, you will find yourself living a freer, more organized life.

■ Perfectionism is not your goal. We mustn't let the excellent become the enemy of the good. Stay focused on the big picture.

> **Organization is 95% making decisions.**

■ Invest wisely in the proper tools for your newly organized life. Quality file cabinets, the right household cleaners, and the appropriate tools are all essential to being organized. You wouldn't try to change a car tire without a jack, would you? On the other hand, many organization gizmos are just that—gizmos. Being able to store more stuff in a closet won't make that closet more organized. It'll just make it more full of stuff.

■ Being organized allows you to set your priorities in order — in the order you want. You won't be ruled by your circumstances; instead, you'll rule them. By having determined your priorities you will be better able to focus on the things that matter to you.

■ You will probably find that as you become more organized, you can actually save money. No more buying another pack of AA batteries because you can't find the rest of the four-pack you know you bought last month.

Is Getting My Life Organized Even Possible?
Applying the ten principles outlined in this book may look like a lot of work at first, but the results will be worth the effort. After a few weeks you'll find yourself applying them with very little thought.

Organization is not an overnight thing. Organizing your life will take some time. You'll be working to develop new thinking patterns and skills. Allowing yourself time to internalize the changes you are trying to make will increase the likelihood of permanent change.

You will have to be willing to do some homework each week. The more you do, the more expertise you will develop at being organized. If you don't put into practice what you are trying to learn, this book will not be very helpful. Just as reading a diet book will not make you thin, I am sorry to report that just reading this book will not make you organized. You are going to have to make yourself organized.

■ Organized living is not about rigid structure or inflexibility. It is about discovering what works in your life, and discarding or changing the rest. You are in control of this process.
You may have to ask yourself some difficult questions and will probably have to change some of your habits.

■ Acting on what you're learning is imperative.

■ Stick with it! The results are well worth the effort!

Putting Away Negatives

We must learn to envision our successes in order to help them happen. Begin by thinking of yourself as becoming more organized. Say to yourself, "I am becoming more organized every day," rather than criticize yourself with mental speech such as "You lost your keys again, you idiot," or "You're so disorganized it is a miracle you don't lose your head sometimes."

> Just as reading a diet book will not make you thin, just reading this book will not make you organized. **You** are going to have to make yourself organized.

Numerous studies have proven the power of positive thinking. Negative thinking has the same power over us to fulfill its prophecy. Don't succumb to negative self-talk. If it helps to write, "I am becoming more organized every day" on 3x5 cards and post them throughout the house, do so. They will also serve as reminders to reinforce the new habits you will be developing.

To help motivate yourself on this journey, visualize the end result of your working to become more organized for the next six weeks. Think of a closet that is functional, not crammed. A briefcase that's orderly with everything in its place. Files that actually help you locate information. You can make significant changes and progress. And once you begin seeing the positive changes, you will be even more motivated to continue to learn more organization skills.

Myths Surrounding Organization

Have you fallen prey to myths that make you feel hopeless? Some common myths about organization are listed below. You can probably add some of your own to this list.

> 'More' is almost never the solution to an organization problem. 'Less' may be the best approach.

If I just had a bigger house [or office], I'd be able to get organized

The truth is, anyone can become more organized. Having more space to spread your disorganization around in usually results only in bigger areas of chaos. Nature abhors a vacuum. And if you're messy with a 5'x 6' cubicle, odds are, you'll be messy in a 12'x12' cubicle, too.

If I had more [shelves, closets, time] I'd be more organized

Again, adding more space to an organization nightmare without solving the underlying organizational problem, will only offer a short-term solution. Unless you increase your organization skills along with your space, the result will still be a larger problem spread over a bigger area.

Time isn't the answer, either, although sometimes we are certain it is. If your time management system isn't functioning well, you are not in control of your days and weeks. Adding more time without solving the underlying time management/organization problem will only result in your wasting greater quantities of time.

I'm just a disorganized person
I am convinced there is no organization gene. Organization is a skill. Like any skill, it takes practice and work to master. But you can learn it and make it part of your daily life. You are probably relatively competent in many areas of your life. You may even be quite organized in many areas of your life. The trick will be learning how to strengthen your organization skills and then translate those skills from one area to another.

Organization is neat
Some people focus a lot of energy on external appearances. But the truth is, an extremely organized and effective person may have a desk that looks like a rat's nest. There is no uniform "look" of organization. The key is determining the level of organization and orderliness that lets you accomplish that which you set out to do. The most important thing about any organization system is that it works for its creator. Thus, your picture of an effective kitchen may not be an uninterrupted expanse of empty counter surfaces, but rather a deliberate collection of the items you use most in the most logical places, even if it does mean you leave appliances out in full view all the time.

> There is no uniform "look" of organization.

The Pareto Principle or The 80-20 Rule
The Pareto Principle is one of the most fundamental concepts in organization. To state it concisely, "Eighty percent of the value comes from 20 percent of the resources." Rather than trying to explain this principle, here are a few examples:

In your closet, 80% of your outfits are probably made up from about 20% of your favorite, most comfortable clothes.

You may have 40 icons on your computer desktop, but probably use only four or five of those programs every day.

In the kitchen, 80% of your meals come from 20% of the items you keep in the pantry. You probably have dozens of spices, but use two or three most consistently.

> There are some tools that provide maximum benefit, and others that are rarely utilized.

In your office you use 20% of the space intensively, the rest only sporadically. Thus the majority of your productivity in the office comes from a few square feet, probably the area in and around your desk and computer.

I've even heard the principle applied to committees—20 percent of the people do 80% of the work. I really can't disagree on that assessment.

The ratio may not be exactly 80-20, but you probably get the idea. In nearly every area of our lives there are some tools or resources that provide maximum benefit, and others that are rarely utilized. The smaller portion (supposedly 20%) you use the most is your critical area of concern.

The good news is that you don't have to get your life 100% organized. This book will try to help you focus on getting your critical 20% organized, so that the 80% productivity will flow smoothly. This goal applies to everything from where you keep your stapler on your desk to how to arrange your closet. By thinking about and applying this fundamental concept to most areas of your life, you will find yourself more organized and effective in the areas that matter most.

2

The Ten Principles of Organization

Just as with any field of knowledge, there are basic principles that can be applied to organization. Listed below are ten of the most important principles you can apply to an area of chaos in your life. In some situations, you may find yourself applying several principles at once. Other times, only one principle may apply. We'll go through these quickly now, with some illustrations to help you anchor them in your mind. Later we'll apply them to various aspects of everyday life.

Decide

Most disorganization can be traced to postponed or unmade decisions. Sometimes we simply don't want to be bothered with making a decision. If you delay deciding something, you may spare yourself what may be a momentarily unpleasant task, but it will more than likely come back to haunt you later. For example, the question "Where should I put the W-2s?" calls for an immediate decision. By not deciding, they end up on the coffee table, the kitchen counter, the night stand, and the dining room table. By April 13th, when you are looking for them, they are buried under four month's debris in five locations around your house.

> Most disorganization can be traced to postponed or unmade decisions.

Addressing decision-making with junk mail is very simple. A catalogue arrives in the mail. Decide: Am I looking for new [whatever is in the catalogue]? If the answer is no, toss the catalogue. If the answer is yes, browse the catalogue quickly and make another decision: Are the items in line with what I am looking for? If no, toss the catalogue. If yes, put it in your "catalogues to browse later" file. And be realistic—not every catalogue that comes into your home needs to go into your browse stack! Decide quickly and you'll find your life a lot less overrun with catalogues.

The same postponed decisions can clog your work and social life, too. An invitation arrives in the mail, but you're not sure you want to commit. You stick the invitation on the refrigerator, where, every time your eye falls on it, it adds stress to your life. You are reminded that you haven't decided to attend (or regret) an event that you are not really looking forward to. By deciding quickly and immediately phoning your regrets to the hostess, you can toss the invitation and be free from ever thinking about it again.

> The same postponed decisions can clog your work and social life, too.

At work most of us have to decide quickly about things. In many cases, other people are waiting on us. In some cases, though, others will wait, pausing their work while we ponder things endlessly. How to make quicker, better decisions at work? Realize that doing nothing is a decision.

If we are fearful of a bad decision, we may hesitate before making one. This delay gives us an illusion of safety. "I haven't botched up the ad campaign by choosing the wrong logo." But in truth, not choosing is a decision. By avoiding the possibility of choosing the wrong logo by postponing the decision, you may really botch the ad campaign by destroying its timeliness.

For some folks, work decisions come easily, but home decisions cause endless hand-wringing. Not making decisions at home turns into quick chaos. And perhaps because we feel safest at home, we're likely to tolerate more chaos. Unmade decisions abound. What to cook for dinner? Can't decide, therefore nothing gets defrosted and you wind up eating out. Again. It seems minor, but the cost of this minor chaos adds up in terms of time away from home, wearing your "public manners," credit card bills and expanding waistlines.

How to decide? Sit down once a week and create a menu. Go ahead and make quick decisions—if it is not fit for a five-star restaurant, no big deal—and you can always select another menu next week. But making the decision in advance takes the pressure off you—you don't have to re-decide every evening.

> Get in the habit of asking yourself, "What is the worst possible thing that could happen to me if I throw this out and later need it again?"

If in doubt, throw it out

This concept might be my favorite organization principle. I know it is the one that produces the greatest peace in my life. While it applies to most aspects of your life, it is especially valuable when applied to paper. If you are looking at a blanket memo that conveys information you already know, just pitch the memo in the trash. Ditto with unworn clothing, weird metallic pieces in your kitchen drawer and nearly expired taco shells you probably won't eat. The best way to apply this principle is to get in the habit of asking yourself, "What is the worst possible thing that could happen to me if I throw this out and later need it again?" In the vast majority of cases, the answer is nothing. You might have to go ask for a copy of that memo from the secretary who sent it. Maybe you have to make a trip to the hardware store for a metal doohickey to replace the one you tossed. Usually the worst-case scenario is not only very unlikely to happen, even if it does, we're talking minor inconvenience, not the end of the world. Get in the habit of purging all non-essential items immediately. You'll be amazed at the sense freedom you gain.

This principle applies to other aspects of your life as well. Do you have a friendship that, while it was once joyful, has become a burden? You find yourself screening his or her phone calls and feeling exhausted when you don't. Maybe it is time to go your separate ways. Are you still a member of the track club, even though your running shoes haven't been used in years? This might offer another opportunity to "throw" something out of your life.

At work we think mostly of papers—but when you're evaluating things to throw out, don't forget emails. Do you have somewhere along the line of 4,867 messages in your in-box? If so, you need to do some weeding. If you've been keeping emails for future reference, make it a point to sort the important ones into appropriate files. Then, those that are left dangling in your inbox can be automatically deleted after a set period of time. Some email programs do this purging automatically.

From the pantry to the garage you'll likely find hundreds of "doubtfuls" in your home. How do you tell? It is easy. You know the keepers—those things that you know you want to keep no matter the cost or hassle of storage or maintenance. If you have to play a scene in your mind attempting to visualize a case where you might use an item—you are experiencing doubt, this is doubt, a good indication that it is time to let it go.

> **If you have to play a scene in your mind to visualize a case where you might use an item—you are experiencing doubt—a good indication that it is time to let it go.**

Bonus Principle: If in doubt, don't buy it

The best way to address excess anything is not to add it to your life to begin with. When you are considering a purchase, ask yourself, "Where will I use this? Where will I store it when I am not using it? Is it likely to end up in a garage sale? How often will I use it in the next three years?"

When you have to wrap your mind around a purchase and imagine a future use, you probably don't need the item. For example, you see an almost new chain saw at a great price at a garage sale.
"Cool. A chain saw! I could use one of these. Let's see—one day that tree in front of the house might grow up to be big enough to need its limbs trimmed. Then there's the chance it might blow down in a

storm. Yeah. A chain saw will be good to have on hand." If this is the internal conversation you have in your head—a potential use that is years down the road—you don't need a chain saw.

Don't buy things for grandkids you don't have yet. Don't buy party supplies for a party you have not planned yet. Don't buy things because they are a good price, smell good, look good, are well-built or for any other enticing reason.

Only buy an item when you have a real need for it and have a place to store it when you are not using it.

Use it or lose it

How many items are you warehousing in your office and home? Are there items that you haven't used recently and are unlikely to ever use again? A good rule of thumb with most items: If you haven't used it in a year, odds are you can live without it. Yes, there are exceptions. You don't have to send all the camping gear to Goodwill just because you didn't use it last summer. But if you know that you hate camping, and only did it to show the kids how to rough it, maybe it is time to purge the gear.

> Don't buy things because they are a good price, smell good, look good, are well-built or for any other enticing reason.

Try the "Have I used it in a year?" question on the contents of your home. If you've got pots, pans, clothes, books, furniture—whatever—cluttering up your life, put it to the use test. If you're not using it, prepare to "lose" it. (Our other principles will help with this.)

Point of use is critical

Do you know many people who keep their office phone in their bottom desk drawer? Probably not. Most people prefer to keep the phone handy. Some even subconsciously place the phone on the side of their "good ear." This is a great example of the point of use principle. Items used every day must be kept in places where they are accessible and easy to use.

Unfortunately, after the telephone, people sometimes don't do so well at keeping things handy. Are there items you find yourself looking for again and again? If the answer is yes, you know you need to relocate those items to more functional places, which may mean taking an inventory of the items you keep in your prime space and making some deletions. For example, if you frequently find yourself reaching for a phone directory at work, it may mean a closer, more convenient place would be helpful. No room you say? I suspect that if you purged your desk drawers of files on dead and/or completed projects, you'd have the space for the directory.

> Items used every day must be kept in places where they are accessible and easy to use.

Again, point of use is critical, and if you're using valuable real estate at work to store dead files, you're not employing this principle.

Recall the Pareto Principle. If you get 80% of your productivity from 20% of the items you keep near you at work, you really want to make sure you have the best 20% at hand.

Here's how to apply this principle. If you have items you use regularly, figure out how many movements they are away for use. For example, you keep your pens in your top drawer. Left hand opens, right hand reaches, and you are ready to write. That's two reaches away. Not bad. If you had to swivel your chair, scoot back, open a drawer, grab a pen, swivel your chair back and scoot back to your desk, that's not good. This principle sounds like common sense, and it is. But it is also very easy to let things wind up in awkward places accidentally. Plan to relocate things while you make your life more organized.

What about non-thing things? For instance, a gym membership at a gym that is close to your last job—but 45 minutes from your new one? That's too far away to be really useful, unless you happen to have an extra 90 minutes in your day for the extra commute.

Is your church far from home? It may be the best fit for your family. But if distance is really getting in the way of your participation in church life, maybe something needs to be changed. The best organization in the world isn't useful if you don't participate in its programs.

You can also apply this principle to your computer files. Do you have to use your "find" command once or more each week? You've got a point of use problem. Are there files you use over and over for an intense period of time? If so, you have probably learned to put them on your desktop—or some other convenient place. But do you make it a point to relocate them to better archival positions once you are not using them as often? Don't give up valuable real estate to dead files—whether it is desk space or virtual space.

Point of use is also critical for a smoothly operating home. I'll share some real life examples from my home. First, I have ugly office-style trash cans in almost every room. Why? Because I want to be able to throw things away now. I know that if I stack a bunch of things neatly to be discarded later, it is very likely these things will end up "inter-stacked" with things I want to keep and I'll have to re-sort the whole stack at some future point. I also keep scissors in a drawer in almost every room.

> Don't give up valuable real estate to dead files—whether it is desk space or virtual space.

I keep Windex™ in every bathroom, the kitchen, and the laundry room. I use it a lot and know I am more likely to keep things tidy if I can just grab the Windex™ and go. I also keep white paper towels nearby. Other things I keep handy are spices and cooking utensils. I want them to be no more than 2 reaches away from the task. (I really do not like to cook and if I make it any more of a chore than it is, I enjoy it even less.)

Handle it once

Do you find yourself moving things around and around your workspace and home? Does it seem that you sort and shuffle stacks of papers repeatedly? If this is the case, you are probably handling things too many times. Try to develop the habit of handling things just one time. For example, when you finish using a power tool, put it away. Avoid setting it on the workbench "for now." Go ahead and put it where it belongs. Otherwise, it will likely wind up buried beneath 12 other objects that get added to the workbench "for now."

> The deadly "for now" causes chaos in many lives.

The deadly "for now" causes chaos in many lives. Develop the habit of sorting the mail once. [Decide.] Move the clean laundry once—i.e., fold it when it comes out of the dryer rather than toss it on the dining room table, the bed or the couch, where after several days it is so wrinkled you have to wash it all over. "For now" is often just a code word for "more work."

This concept is especially critical when it comes to papers. When a paper enters your life, learn to deal with it immediately. It may seem like a time saver to set a sheet aside to deal with later, but more often than not, you'll find yourself with an 'In Basket' that remains full, causing you to shuffle through it several times a week to find things.

What about meetings? Are you discussing the same meeting topics over and over? If every committee meeting seems to be re-hashing the same old issues, you may be "handling" an issue too many times without really addressing it. Could it be that a postponed decision is bogging things down? If "old business" remains the predominant focus of every meeting, you'll need to find ways to speed up decision-making. This acceleration could involve anything from inviting people of greater authority, who can address the problem, or deciding the problem has no ready solution and moving on.

Set limits

To control clutter, chaos and excess, set a maximum number and stick to it. Do you collect penguins? Decide that you will never keep more than 25 at a time. When holidays result in your collection growing, weed out the less desirable penguins until you are at your target number. You can also loudly announce at Thanksgiving that you no longer collect penguins, thank you. (I used this on my accidental duck collection. It worked.)

Do you find yourself keeping nice boxes for gift-wrapping? Set a limit, say 4 boxes, and stick to it. When a new box comes into your life, compare it to the others and keep the best four. The same methodology can be applied to those nifty string-handled gift bags and shopping bags.

What about social events? You might decide for peace of mind to never schedule more than two social events during any single weekend. By setting the limit, you don't have to re-decide every time your calendar starts to fill up. After accepting the first two invitations, you simply say, "I'm so sorry, but I'm all booked up the weekend of the 8th. Thank you for inviting me. I'm sorry I'll miss all the fun." This technique also works on volunteer activities and church committee assignments.

I know of one family who, in the interest of getting to see their own children on a semi-regular basis, decided to limit extracurricular activities to one per semester. Were these "deprived" children able to recover from this arbitrary limitation on their lives? Yes. In fact, both went to a private college on full scholarship.

> Limits are a paradox. With limits you gain freedom, because limits protect you from enslavement to "too many" or "too much."

The freedom here is that no one is told they cannot save rubber bands, pretty string-handled bags, or mayonnaise jars. They can keep them forever if they wish. But, they can only keep a set number and excess gets recycled. Chaos is controlled, and the collector is happy.

Determine a place for everything

This problem area is where postponed decisions have made your life miserable. When you haven't already decided, once and for all, exactly where you are going to keep items, you end up looking for them repeatedly. Decide on a proper location for each item.

An example I see all the time: women digging through their purses for their car keys. (Sorry to stereotype, but it is true. And it can be a safety issue if your distraction makes you vulnerable to predators.) Anything you go hunting for again and again needs the application of this principle. Going back to our first principle, decide where you will keep your car keys. Decide once and for all that no matter which purse or briefcase you use, your keys will always be put in the same place—say the outermost pocket. There. Put them back each time until a habit is formed and now you know where your keys are every time. Even if you switch to a backpack for a day hike, using the "place for everything" principle, you can put the keys in your pre-determined place, the outermost pocket, and know where they are.

> When you haven't already decided, once and for all, exactly where you are going to keep items, you end up looking for them repeatedly. Decide on a proper location for each item.

Where do you store your extra office supplies? Or your vacuum cleaner? The vinegar? Your VISA card? If your answers to these questions vary with the phase of the moon, plan to decide now where you are going to keep items. As you finish using them, stop and consider, "Where is the most logical place to keep this item?" Bear in mind the point of use principle. You don't want to keep the kitty litter stored 30 feet from the cat box. One way to determine where to put something is to ask yourself, "Where would I look for this item first?" As you determine proper locations for things, steadfastly return them to their proper places until a habit is established.

This idea even works for appointments if you will determine the place to track them is your calendar. If you've set good limits and you have a "place" for all your events, a glance at your calendar (you do have one, right?) will tell you if you can accept a new obligation.

Recycle, reuse, release

As you get better and better with your decision-making skills, you are going to find yourself with a problem: what to do with that which you do not want or need.

> There are more ways to recycle than to put things in to color-coded bins.

Recycling is very popular now. But there are more ways to recycle than to put things in to color-coded bins. As you consider your home and work spaces, are there objects that no longer have a productive use for you? If you no longer enjoy something, or it no longer adds utility to your life, consider getting rid of it.

There are many ways to "recycle" things. A good habit to develop is to give things away freely. Let's consider the purple cow creamer Aunt Martha gave you. You never liked it, but your neighbor collects cows. Pass it on. You'll enjoy having it out of our life, and your neighbor will be tickled at the kitschy addition to her collection.

Giving at work can mean returning to the supply cabinet office supplies that clog your desk drawers. Or passing along the never-used transcription equipment to someone else.

Of course, there is always Goodwill and The Salvation Army and even those handy color-coded bins. The idea is to begin thinking about what you can delete from your life painlessly. It is probably more than you realize.

We all enjoy some traditions. But there are times when a tradition outlives its usefulness. Has a tradition become a meaningless chore for you? If so, here is a chance to creatively "recycle" the tradition into something that is more meaningful to the people involved.

One family I know had several members involved in retail management—which meant from the day after Thanksgiving to early January a family gathering was out of the question. So they moved Christmas to the summer. Why not? It is not illegal to put up a Christmas tree in July. (You might want to hold off on the exterior decorations, depending on your neighborhood covenants.)

I got a delightful family newsletter in September this year. It was such a pleasure to read and it didn't get tossed—unread—into a stack of Christmas cards. I thought it was a great idea. To "recycle" the newsletter from the holiday season to a time when life is less hectic made the newsletter more enjoyable to both the writer and the reader.

> Hold onto things with a loose grip. The harder we cling to something, the more work it becomes.

Another recycling method is to use objects for purposes other than those for which they were intended. If you have a number of lovely crystal vases that remain unseen and unappreciated in a closet, why not use one as a pencil holder? Your old golf bag with built in cart could be a handy yard tool caddy. The point is, don't be a warehouse; either use an item, or give it to a good home that will.

The ultimate point behind this principle is to hold onto things with a loose grip. The harder we cling to something, the more work it becomes. One of my class members shared a great idea that illustrates a loose grip: throwing a rock at her car.

You know how when you get a new car you tend to be meticulous about taking care of it? Maybe you haven't done it, but I have—sometimes going to extremes of parking in the outermost parking spaces to avoid those inevitable nicks and bumps the paint will suffer.

My student would throw a rock at her new car, thereby eliminating the agony of trying to avoid the first ding. That's a loose grip, and a much more peaceful position than the anxiety-filled "pre-ding" mind-set.

Do one more thing

As you leave an area, consider what "one more thing" you could do to make re-entry into that area easier when you return. As you leave the kitchen, what five-second action could make things better when you return? Wiping the jelly off the counter before it turns to hard goo? Rinsing the sink? Putting the cereal away? Or maybe even getting the cereal out for breakfast the next morning.

At your work place, about five minutes before you leave, pause to do one more thing that will make your arrival at work easier the next day. Could you jot down a list of top priorities? What about pulling out the file for the project you will begin in the morning?

Think in terms of small, concrete steps you can take that will make re-entry easier. If you make it a habit to do one more thing each time you move from one activity to another, you will find you've already begun your task when you return to the office, or kitchen, or whatever. This method will make re-entry easier, focus you more readily on the next task at hand, and reduce the "dreads." Really, who wants to face a kitchen with hardened grape jelly cemented to the counter?

> If you make it a habit to do one more thing each time you move from one activity to another, you will find you've already begun your task when you return.

Don't collect junk

Become extremely picky about what elements of your life you keep. Life is too short to clutter it with junk. Junk can be odd mementos given to you by well-meaning friends, outdated or uncomfortable furniture, itchy (but expensive) sweaters or other objects that no longer bring you pleasure. Junk can even be bad relationships that only depress you and deplete your energy.

Start now by eliminating the things in your life you just don't like. Never liked houseplants, but people gave you several when you were sick? Give them away or put them out of their misery.

> **Eliminate the things in your life you just don't like.**

There is more junk at work than the odds and ends in your desk drawer. What about useless assignments? Extra committee appointments? Meetings to plan meetings? At one organization I am affiliated with there was once a Committee on Committees! Doesn't that sound like fun?

Unless you are the CEO, you can't really jettison work assignments at your own will, but you can take up the discussion, tactfully, with your boss if too many non-essential tasks are impeding your work on priority projects.

Try to view your home and office with a critical eye, as if you had never stepped foot in the door before. You may enjoy offbeat décor, and that's fine. But is there anything downright tacky present? If so, relieve yourself of the burden.

And then there's "Junque." Do you have antique furniture that no one can sit in because it is too fragile? It is junque. Pristine white carpet in a room no one's allowed to walk in? Junque. Just because it is expensive, valuable or pretty doesn't ensure worth. If it adds to chaos in your life—or just headache and hassle—it is really junk.

Does the Bovine Club membership you keep no longer bring you fun and fellowship? Maybe it is time to resign. Sometimes purging your life of a time worn object or commitment can be scary. Purging something will leave a vacuum, and most people usually strenuously avoid vacuums. But consider this: a vacuum can be a place of peace and serenity. And just because a vacuum may exist in your living room when you get rid of the ugly orange chair, you don't have to rush right out and get a new one. Live with the vacuum a while, and then decide what you want (if anything) for that space in your life. It may well be that the peace you feel from ridding yourself of burdensome objects may more than compensate for the loss of a chair.

Then there is another kind of junk altogether. It is the emotional-strings-attached junk that insinuates itself into your life. One day in my organization class, a woman had tears in her eyes as she described a painful pressure point in her home. Her mother-in-law had given her a large, fragile, blown glass sculpture. It was kept in the living room. Not only was it not to the woman's tastes—its delicacy meant her three small boys were essentially banned from that room.

She felt this ugly (but expensive) sculpture was holding a good portion of her home hostage. My advice? Break it! That may sound harsh, but after talking to this woman for several minutes, there seemed to be no other solution. So I suggested she let her kids play around in the room in hopes an errant toss would take out the sculpture. (I might have simply dropped in on a tile floor myself.) Breaking this item may sound extreme—but the mother-in-law wasn't about to let it be put into storage.

> There is another kind of junk altogether. It is the emotional-strings-attached junk that insinuates itself into your life.

They couldn't sell it at a garage sale. And the mother-in-law wasn't exactly ancient, either, so they could not bear the thought of simply trying to outlive her.

To liberate herself from the emotional control her mother-in-law exerted, breakage seemed a worthwhile choice. After all, what could the mother-in-law do upon hearing the sculpture was broken (to smithereens)? Kill a grandson? Not likely. Buy a new one? She probably would not trust them with a new sculpture after the careless breakage. Would she get mad? Probably. But we had established that she was already going to get mad with every other possible removal scenario. At least this scenario had the mother-in-law getting mad and the offending sculpture gone. You'd hate to put the thing in storage, have a family feud over it, and then be forced to put the horrid thing back on display.

This example leads to my next point about junk. Be very careful from whom you accept "gifts." If Aunt Lucinda is going to go berserk if you re-cover her divan, don't accept it unless you love its upholstery.

Consider the giver's track record. Does this person ever "check up" on the status or location of gifts? Does she ask you where things she gave you are? Has she ever asked any family member to return a gift? If so—don't accept things from this person unless you really want it, love it, and intend to keep it (pristine) for the rest of the giver's natural life.

How to say no? Try telling the giver that you simply don't think you'd be a good steward of such a "valuable" item. If that doesn't work, try the truth—you don't want it. She may get mad. Given her track record of strings-attached giving, she was likely to wind up mad at some point or other anyway.

3

The Foundation of Organization: Clutter Removal

Okay, you've read the ten principles. Now it is time to put them to use. Following the simple instructions below and using the ten principles, you are ready to conquer some chaos. Read through the entire exercise, schedule your assignment (see Appendix A for complete instructions) and start getting organized.

Supplies needed:

Block of time alone. Go ahead and schedule a time several days out. Write it down in your calendar. This interval gives you mental preparation time. Arrange for privacy. Serious de-cluttering doesn't lend itself to an audience.

Four to seven medium cardboard boxes. Boxes stand up and so they are best. Plastic garbage bags may be substituted for some of the boxes.

Label the boxes as follows:
1. Garbage
2. Give away (Salvation Army)
3. Relocate (not mine, not here!)
4. Doubt
5. Alter or repair
6. Borrowed and need to be returned

Step One:

Select a well-defined area of chaos to start on—something concrete with clear boundaries, such as the closet or the car, or maybe just a tabletop or desktop. Don't attempt to conquer the entire house in your first session or you'll wind up discouraged at the magnitude of the task.

Now, set up your sorting boxes. And don't forget the 'privacy' you'll need. You won't get far on this if you have a screaming audience wailing over every item you try to purge.

> Don't attempt to conquer the entire house in your first session or you'll wind up discouraged at the magnitude of the task.

Keeping the ten Principles in mind, quickly go through the area, placing items in the appropriate box. For things that belong in the area you are de-cluttering and organizing, set them aside neatly, so you can return them to their places when you are finished.

It is best to go quickly. Trust your first judgment and keep moving. Studiously apply the ten principles. If your "Doubt" box fills up first, you are not deciding—you are postponing decisions.

Step Two:
After everything is sorted, go through the Doubt box with a hard heart and sort it into the other boxes. Sort every item into the other boxes. You have to resolve your doubts now.

Step Three:
Next, deal with the Alter or Repair box. Are you really going to have the work done? If the truthful answer is no, get rid of these items, too. If you really will invest the time and money on the repair, make a plan for it to happen. If it involves a trip to the repair shop or alteration shop, jot these on your calendar or to do list. Or delegate them to another family member.

Step Four:
After everything is sorted, take the boxes to the appropriate place. Do

not stack the boxes in the garage or carport. Do not cram them in a closet. Make it a point to deal with them.

Throw away the garbage box today. Take it out to the curb, even if trash collection isn't for three more days. If your family seems overly curious or concerned about the contents of the garbage box, take it to a dumpster, put it in front of a neighbor's house—anything to keep your family from picking through the box and digging out treasures.

Deliver the "Relocate" box to the proper rooms. If they are open, take the charity box to Goodwill, Salvation Army, etc. Or put it in your car for delivery the next day. If you really plan to fix the broken vacuum cleaner, put it in the car, maybe even the front seat. Keep it visible (and irritating), so you will be forced to do something about it. Do not stash the seven "Repair" items in a closet and pretend they do not exist. We are trying to reduce chaos, not add to it. As for the borrowed items, put them in your vehicle as well. If you have time, start returning them today. If you do not have time, make an appointment in your calendar to return the borrowed items this week.

> **Make sure your most-used items occupy the 20% hot zone.**

Step Five:

Now, put the remainders back in their proper places, using the ten principles. Make sure your most-used items occupy the 20% hot zone. For a linen closet, this means the most used items at easy reach level. The extra pillows for the seldom-used guest bedroom can be higher up. You get the idea.

Before you read this chapter, do the de-cluttering exercise mentioned at the end of Chapter One. For best results, consult Appendix A and spend some time developing a strategy to take you through the next few weeks of your organization process. Even if you don't have the time to evaluate your situation and develop priorities, it is important to complete at least one "de-cluttering." That experience will make the content of this chapter more meaningful.

4

It's Not As Easy As It Sounds, Is It?

Most of us consider ourselves to be rational beings, making decisions based upon well-thought-out ideas and plans. At times, however, we rationalize our way into a clutter-keeping trap. The biggest problem I hear about from my students is getting rid of things. They add things to their throw away box, then they sneak an item or two back out. For every two that go in, one comes back out. Finally, some decide it is hopeless and come to class and try to convince me they absolutely had to save the items they kept. Below are some of the things they tell me. Do any of the following rationalizations sound familiar to you?

"This might really come in handy someday"

The number one protest I hear in my organization class is, "But I might need it someday!" Yes, you might. But then again, you might not. If you think about the unlimited possibilities of life, virtually every object you ever touch might be theoretically needed "someday." Do you really plan to keep everything you ever touch? Of course not.

So ask yourself... On that imaginary day when you actually need this item again, what will happen if you don't have it? Will it be life or death? (Keep the nitroglycerin tablets!) Or will it be only a mild inconvenience? Or will it not matter at all? That pack of seven birthday candles, for example. Yes, keep them if you have a child under seven. But if all your kids are grown and it is unlikely that you'll ever use just seven birthday candles, go ahead and toss them. If you keep them and tell yourself you'll buy more to go with the seven when you need twelve, you'll discover that the new ones don't match the ugly old ones anyway. You'll just toss them back in the drawer where they will be in your way every time you reach for the kitchen scissors. They'll aggravate you until your estate is settled and your executor puts them where they really belong—in the trash!

"This was made back in the days when quality and craftsmanship mattered"

That's probably right. But are you actually using that object's fine quality to enhance your life, or is it just taking up space? You can admire fine workmanship without owning it. (Besides, if it is an old appliance, you'll worry about its safety and never use it anyway for fear its wonderful quality will burn your house down.)

"It reminds me of [something significant]" and other emotional clutter traps

I hate to tell you this, but Granny's not in that lamp! Yes, things do remind you of people you love or places you've enjoyed. But they are only symbols of the people or places they remind you of. Thus, if you discard a pair of miniature wooden clogs, you won't be destroying The Netherlands. And your memories that are triggered by the clogs are held in your heart and head—not in the wooden clogs. So if the wooden clogs no longer bring you daily joy, but instead add to the clutter you must maintain, dust and keep arranged—get rid of them!

If the trinket brings you joy each time your eyes fall upon it, by all means keep it. But if the memories are stale and no longer rewarding, feel free to liberate yourself from the physical symbol. I'd guess that if you are considering letting it go, you are ready to let it go.

On that imaginary day when you actually need this item again, what will happen if you don't have it? Will it be life or death?

A note on gifts: No matter how hurt people are when they find out you've moved (or even discarded) their gift, they really cannot expect to control you for the rest of your life by forcing you to display an object you do not enjoy. You are not betraying that person by getting rid of an object. Your love remains undiminished. Communicate that thought. Keep things out of joy, not guilt.

If you have gift donors who really feel that you are honor-bound to do as they wish with a gift, you have several choices. You can do as you wish, risking alienation from a person who wants to control you (maybe not a bad thing). You can do as you wish and they may never give you anything again (again, maybe not a bad thing). You can refuse to accept gifts with strings attached. Or you can accept the gift gracefully, with full knowledge of the strings attached. If you do accept the gift, you should not harbor ill feelings towards the donor; after all, accepting the gift was your choice.

Overcoming Rationalizations

No one likes an argument, least of all with oneself! But here are a few ideas on combating rationalizations that result in your keeping everything.

One way to "argue" these rationalizations with yourself is to try and put a cost on maintaining the questioned item. If there is only a 1/100th percent chance you will ever need the item again in the next decade, is it worth 3,650 days of living with it, moving it around, dusting it, air-conditioning it, and keeping track of it? Probably not.

Another question to ask is what percentage of your life will you devote to storing excess clutter? If ten percent of your home is filled with clutter, is it worth ten percent of your mortgage payment to continue to warehouse it? How many hours must you work for the dollar amount you are investing in needless storage? If that amount seems insignificant, get a finance person to calculate its future value. That will be eye opening when you consider that amount invested in your retirement rather than the mini-warehouse you'll eventually need. (If you don't already have one now.)

A third question to ask yourself is this: If I persist in keeping this stuff, what will happen to it when I die? Odds are very strong that your heirs will send most of it to Goodwill without as much as a loving glance. Half-finished projects, old catalogues, eight-track tapes—all of this "stuff" will wind up either in a landfill or on the shelves of a thrift store.

The final word.

Now or later, your clutter will be dealt with!

You can sort it now. Choosing how and when to disperse or dispose of it.

You can wait until you are aged and infirm and try to deal with it when you break up housekeeping.

> **Now or later, your clutter will be dealt with!**

Or you can leave the problem to others and let your heirs plunder through it. But don't ever doubt that one day everything will be dealt with. You cannot take it with you.

5

Calendars

If you hope to be at all organized and to integrate the various elements of your life, a calendar is indispensable. Nothing can replace a good calendar.

Should it be electronic or paper? Should it live on your desktop computer or in your Personal Digital Assistant? Only you know for sure, and it may take you several trials to see what works for you.

I have used a large 8 1/2x11 inch Day Timer®, a Palm Pilot, generic calendars from Office Depot and even wall calendars. But I've used each of these at different points in my life. When I was in charge of a big project at work, I went to the large Day Timer® because I needed lots of space. During this period of my life I was on 12 different work-related committees. The Day Timer® was huge but effective. I left it at work on a special podium designed just for it—to keep it always visible. I seldom took it home and that was not much of a problem. During this period of my life my after-work time was mostly spent in sheer exhaustion—I didn't need a calendar to record home-life activities—I wasn't having any!

Your calendar needs will likely be different at different points in your life.

This period of my life passed (as all phases do) and I graduated to a Palm Pilot. It fit nicely in my purse, had all the phone numbers I could ever possibly need, and worked great as a schedule book, too. I used it for a number of years. But then life got busier. I went back to a half-sized portfolio calendar that I carry around. I need more space to jot down information (and to do it quickly) so this makes sense, now, in this phase of my life.

Your calendar needs will likely be different at different points in your life. I'd buy less expensive calendars until you find what works for you. If a calendar is not working, go and buy another style. Time is too precious to squander on a bad calendar.

Your calendar should be big enough to write in all necessary details. A birthday party on Saturday? You'll need time and place—and maybe even the honoree's name. Make it a point to put as much information in the calendar as you need. Don't just say "party" and then scramble around for the invitation Saturday morning.

> **If you have a calendar, but fail to note things on it, you really just have a paperweight.**

Examples of details you should make a point to note: Date, day and time of meeting, length of meeting, topic, and what items you should take with you.

Your calendar should foster communication across various aspects of your life. By this I mean you should be able to record all sorts details from various parts of your life, such as church, home and work on it. A calendar you carry it with you does this easily. So does an Internet-based calendar, since you have access to it from almost any location. If you have a calendar, but fail to note things on it, you really just have a paperweight.

When you use a calendar remember to schedule into your life periods of time to get your own stuff done. If you need two hours twice a week to write, schedule them in. Use ink!

6

Dealing With Paper Using the Ten Principles

You've heard of a "paper tiger," haven't you? It is a phrase used to describe something that appears to be bigger than it appears. There's even a great book entitled *Conquering the Paper Tiger: Organizing the Paper in Your Life*, by Barbara Hemphill. Paper clutter is a good example of something that can appear monstrous, but when cut down to size, it is mere, well...paper.

Let's be honest: paper ranks right up there with Death and Taxes. There will even be paperwork after our demise for our descendants to handle. That notion of the "paperless" society didn't take into account the human tendency to make two (or more) copies now that technology is so accessible. (Let's face it, who among us hasn't printed out an e-mail message?)

In dealing with paper problems, it is best to take a multi-faceted approach. Eliminate paper at its source, attack the incoming stream, and then conquer the backlog.

Let's take a minute and run through the ten principles with just paper in mind.

Decide

Like most disorganization, paper problems are really postponed decisions. Learning to make quick decisions the first time you encounter a piece of paper is critical. The first decision to make about paper is, does it even belong to you? If the paper is someone else's to worry about—just send it on its way. Don't waste any more time or energy on other folks' papers.

Maybe it is your paper. You get a junk mail solicitation. It sounds interesting. You might go for it. But you don't decide. Instead, you add the new piece of junk mail to your pile of 7,569 other pieces of junk mail. Then you wonder why you have "stuff" stacked all over the house. We must learn to not postpone decisions. Decide what to keep and what to toss. Then actually toss the things that deserve it. (Remember my Point of Use Principle and the trash can in every room?)

If in doubt, throw it out

By asking, "What's the worst thing that will happen to me if I toss this paper?" you will find that many of the annoying items in your life can be quickly dispatched. This principle is really the question part of the Decide principle. If you have to struggle to come up with a reason to keep a piece of paper, it should probably go.

Use it or lose it

This method applies to those papers you already have—the ones scattered all over the place as well as those in a file cabinet. Are you hanging onto files you've never consulted? Do you still have your predecessor's files even though you've held your current position ten years and never once consulted those files? It is been reported that 80% of what gets filed in the typical office is never looked at again.

> If you struggle to come up with a reason to keep a piece of paper, it should probably go.

We're just as bad at home. Do you have instruction manuals for appliances you no longer own? If you do, you are fairly normal. Papers for which you have no future use are merely postponed recycling. Lose 'em!

Point of use is critical

In the library world we say, "A mis-shelved book is a lost book." This same thought applies to papers. Papers you can't find when you need them are utterly useless. You might as well not even have them. If you are depending on information in these papers to guide you in your decision-making, it is essential that they be available to you. "Somewhere in the office, in a yellow or green envelope" does not count as accessible. You must learn to file. (More on this later.) Filing is essential follow-through for paper organization. A stack on top of a file cabinet is not filed. Set aside time to put papers away on a regular basis.

Handle it once

Do you find yourself circulating paper around and around your desk, home or car? If so, you have the perfect opportunity to learn to handle papers as little as possible. If you have to handle papers more than once, for example, keeping bills to pay on payday, at the very least you must learn to put them in a place reserved for unpaid bills and nothing else.

> **Papers for which you have no future use are merely postponed recycling. Lose 'em!**

Sound overwhelming? Remember, once you learn to make quick decisions and cull ruthlessly, you'll have a lot fewer papers to handle.

Set limits

To reduce your paper load, set limits on how many papers you'll hang onto. Perhaps you will save only the best of the best of your six-year-old's artistic creations. You're not a bad parent if you only keep 12 art projects from the first grade.

Likewise, how many of your own creations are you hanging onto? Do you have fourth, fifth, and sixth drafts of reports? Set a limit and decide to only keep the number of drafts you might realistically need, maybe only the first and last, or the last two.

Determine a place for everything

Just file it! For the papers you decide to keep, it is imperative that they have a home. Permanent residence in your In Basket does not count. We'll talk more about this matter later, but no matter what, you must invest the time to set up a simple, workable system.

Recycle, reuse, release

Let's be honest, most recycling in this area will have more to do with getting the paper into the recycling bin than with passing papers along to more appropriate parties. However, in workplaces, papers often arrive at your door that belong to others or can be delegated. Learn to pass this paper on immediately.

Do one more thing

This principle leads you to complete one more, small task before you leave an area. Regarding paperwork, what additional small step could you take to complete your handling of a paper item? Could you go ahead and browse the catalogue and then put it in the trash? Could you file the memo you just read? Or toss it? Add information from papers to the place it belongs.

A lot more energy goes into remembering not to throw away a paper than it takes to deal with it properly. In many cases, one small action will ensure that a piece of paper never bothers you again.

If you are hanging onto an opened, crumpled envelope because it has a return address you want to keep—just copy the address into your address book and toss the envelope. After all, sooner or later, you'll lose the envelope. After having protected it and shuffled it for months, you end up without the address, despite all your efforts. A lot more energy goes into remembering not to throw away an envelope than it takes to jot an address in a calendar. In many cases, one small action will ensure that a particular piece of paper never bothers you again.

Don't collect junk

Be extremely critical of any paper you decide to save. Is it really necessary? Will it be outdated in a few weeks? Don't let the habit of saving every little scrap of paper turn your file system into an archive of irrelevant garbage.

7

The Paper Questions

Just as with clutter, there are rationalizations that tend to go along with excess paper retention. To help clarify your decision-making, ask these questions when it comes to paper.

What is the worst thing that could happen to me if I throw this away?

If the answer is nothing. . . Throw it away. If the answer is still pretty mild, "I might have to open a cookbook (that I already have) and look up a recipe for dip," you are probably better off tossing the paper in question.

Where should I keep this piece of paper?

If you cannot live without that recipe for dip, I suggest you copy it into a notebook right now. Not when you get time, not tomorrow. Now. Decide where the proper place for the item is as soon as possible and put it there. Because for me the logical place to keep a recipe I've clipped is with my cookbooks I have sometimes stapled recipes to end papers of cookbooks. I also keep magazine file boxes near my cookbooks to stash Internet recipe printouts or larger pieces of paper as well as flimsy cooking magazines.

Once I put this piece of paper in its proper place, how will I know where to find it again?

We will go over filing tips later, but for now, the best way to decide where to put things is to simply decide, go ahead and create the file folder, box or whatever, and then consistently put like items there until it is a habit. How do you decide? It is easy. Simply ask yourself, Where would I look first if I wanted to locate this paper again?

How long should I keep it?

When you set up a filing for something, you're almost guaranteeing it'll still be in its manila folder when you retire. Before you archive things, make sure you really need them. Are you keeping copies of items that are kept elsewhere in your firm? Is there a later draft of the item in question? If the answers are yes, toss the item you have in front of you. If you decide to keep it, consider putting down a "throw away after" date on the file.

> At home and in the office, determine a single place to deal with your incoming paper. Pick just one place.

Where will I deal with my paper?

At home and in the office, determine a single place to deal with your incoming paper. Pick just one place. Think about getting plastic or wire baskets for this location. Here you will unload all incoming paper: mail, memos, etc. Make sure there is a large trash can within two feet of this place. You want the trash can large enough to swallow a JC Penney® catalogue easily—not one of those wimpy, dainty wastebaskets.

Special Note for Workplaces

Here again, the key is to follow through. Delegate immediately. Take the actions required as soon as possible. You should go through your "action required" pile at least daily. Set aside time to file those true keepers at least once a week, better yet, twice. Is there so much paper you don't know where to start? We'll talk about backlogs soon. In the meantime, don't let your backlog grow!

Potential paper problems

On the surface, this approach all sounds so simple, because it really is. But beneath simple principles are underlying human tendencies. Do any of the following sound vaguely familiar?

Un-made decisions

You get an announcement from church about a new dinner group that is meeting every other Friday. By Friday all you want to do is crawl under a rock and hide. But you're a nice person. The fellowship offered sounds good; you want to be supportive of the new associate pastor in charge. Ask yourself: Do I want to commit to this event? If the answer is "No," then toss the piece of paper and get over it. Not deciding is a postponed decision! You know postponed decisions result in chaos.

Control Issues

If you put all the 1099s in your husband's basket, are you sure he'll keep track of them? Maybe he'll lose them. So you decide to start your own file for tax papers. Pretty soon no one knows where anything is, because there are conflicting filing systems in place. Decide who will do what, and put the papers in the appropriate place. (If your spouse does lose that paper, the calls necessary to re-create the file will be very educational.)

Gretchen's System:

I have three large wire baskets and a large office-style wastepaper basket. I use this incoming place for a very rough sort of my home papers:

When the mail arrives, I go through it rapidly and toss out any junk mail addressed to me. I leave junk mail addressed to my husband on his placemat. At some point every evening, the stuff all wind up in one of four places.

Basket One: (Gretchen's basket): Bills to pay and things to file or otherwise keep. This location is a temporary place for the "keepable" items. I pay the non-automated bills straight out of this basket.

Basket Two: Things to look at later, — interesting junk mail, catalogues, etc. These things are not retained, and are frequently tossed. If the basket stacks up, I know it can be tossed wholesale into the trash without review.

Basket Three: This basket is where stuff for my husband goes. I toss things in, and it is his responsibility to keep track of what's in here, and where it should be filed later. It sometimes overflows.

Garbage: Some days the only thing I can say I accomplished is to throw out the incoming junk mail. I make it a point to be ruthless. It is a good feeling.

8

Filing Systems

There are basically two types of filing systems. One is for "permanent keepers" (your archives) and the other for your active use files.

Archives

Librarians like file systems. I started out in the Special Collections department of a major university library. There we had old and rare books, as well as the university archives. We deliberately kept the older stuff away from the circulating collection. This concept of having a separate area—away from the wear and tear of daily use—can also be applied to your personal archives. This is where you keep those sentimental things you cannot bear to part with, such as your Valentine's Day card from 1992. Other long-term information is considered historical, too, such as copies of your old tax returns, receipts for home improvements that will help you figure out your basis when you sell the house, and warranties. This material is stuff you seldom consult, but need to keep. Notice no one is saying you can't keep it—even the Valentine's Day card—you just need to put it in a place where it is not in your way as you consult the files you use often.

Active

These are files for active projects, things you refer to on a regular basis. It may be daily or weekly, but it should be at least every other month or so. This category includes files for all active accounts, bills, this year's insurance claims and other active accounts or projects.

Point of Use

Remembering the point of use principle, try to use your prime organizational real estate for your most active current use files. That concept means the projects you are working on right now belong on your desktop. The file you will use to compile your monthly report will go in a desk drawer. Your Archives can be farther away from your primary workspace. Long, long term items (tax papers from several years ago) can be kept in well-labeled file storage boxes in your attic.

Part of conquering the paper mess is setting up a decent filing system. Here's how.

Tools

Let's start with a filing cabinet. If you don't already have one, it will be a good investment. Purchase a quality file cabinet from an office supply or office furniture store. You do not want the cheapest model. Ease of use is critical and if you are struggling with balky drawer slides that don't work, you'll be less inclined to file.

If you are setting up a new file system, consider hanging files. They are easier to use because they keep files from slipping down beneath one another. You can still file your manila file folders inside the hanging files, too, making them perfect for subject groupings.

You'll probably need to purchase the metal hanging file frames for these separately from your filing cabinet, so get them at the same time.

While you're shopping, get plenty of hanging files, plain file folders and any miscellaneous filing supplies you might need—such as alphabetical dividers, if you like them.

Other tools to keep near you as you begin to file are your calendar and your address book. Many papers can be dismissed from your life forever if you just transfer the information to the right place.

Hints on Filing

The best file system is one that works for you. While a purist might insist on strict alphabetical file arrangement, I strongly recommend you group your files in the way that works best for you. If you think of your life in compartments, your files will likely be grouped by compartments. Within each compartment you may use alphabetical arrangements or another grouping.

I tend to keep my files lumped by "home things" and "writing things" in my home office; at the library where I work, I tend to group things alphabetically. At the magazine office, I have three systems: one chronological for everything having to do with issues, one alphabetical (it is more like my archives), and a third thematic—that correlates to how we do our bookkeeping—state tax files, federal tax files, personnel files, etc. It may sound like a waste of time to have three separate filing systems in three different locations in my office, but I really only need the tax files and personnel files when I do payroll, so I don't want them mixed in with my issue files that I plunder through all the time.

> **The best file system is one that works for you.**

Subject Headings

If you can't find it, you don't have it! Assigning subject headings is very important, because once an item is filed, if it is irretrievable due to a bad subject heading, it may as well be tossed out with the recycling. To determine subject headings, ask yourself: Where would I look if I wanted to find this item? What is the term you think of when reflecting on a topic? Do you think of "Metro Power and Light" or "Utilities?" Either one could be right for you. Pick a heading that makes sense to you. I use "Vet," not "North State Animal Hospital."

Use terms that result in reasonable-sized files

Make sure you have enough items to justify a file before you set one up — several items (4 to 6) are needed, otherwise try to fit the papers into an existing, broader heading. It is easier to look through a single file with 15 different pieces of paper than 15 files with a single piece of paper each. When faced with just one or two items, try to think of larger terms to group things together. A heading like "Home Projects" works for me to put away all those odd magazine pages of the perfect kitchen, an ad for some framed prints I like but cannot afford, and a craft idea. I could have used separate files for "Kitchen," "Art Work" and "Crafts" but I knew I wouldn't have very much to go in the three separate headings, and so this broad heading works for me.

Group like things together until you have to break things into separate folders because the file is getting unwieldy. At that point, consider subheadings. I use "Medical" for everything from prescriptions to dentists to eye doctors. The year I had surgery, however, I wound up with a single file just for those papers.

Adjectives, Creative
Never begin a file heading with an adjective. Use, Clients, not New Clients. One day your new clients will be old clients anyway, right? When assigning headings get to the core of the topic. If you use "clients" instead of "new clients" and "long-term clients" all client information ends up together. To gather all your information about all your clients, you can go to one place.

Tackling Backlogs
The best way to think of a paper backlog, especially a serious, multi-year backlog, is as a marathon. It is not a quick sprint; you'll need to do some training to get your paper-processing muscles in shape before you can be successful.

A Word of Caution
If you set up a really neat, easy-to-use file system, be careful that you don't overdo it. I have a tendency to keep everything nearly forever. For example—phone bills back to the month I married. (Finally at our 8th anniversary, I got around to some serious purging.) Just because you have a file for it doesn't mean you have to file a specific item or keep it very long.

If you are like most people, you have a backlog of papers to deal with. Before you tackle a five-year backlog of unfiled papers, stem the incoming tide. Begin by dealing with every paper that crosses your desk or threshold on a daily basis. As you become more skilled in making on-the-spot decisions, you will be better able to begin dealing with the backlog.

I'd give myself a week of daily dealing with paper before I began tackling the backlog. I'd also begin the backlog in small, defined pieces, say, everything on the kitchen counter, rather than declare war on every paper in the house. Defining small concrete areas to tackle is the best way to address paper clutter. If you take on too much, you are setting yourself up for failure.

> **Defining small concrete areas to tackle is the best way to address paper clutter. If you take on too much, you are setting yourself up for failure.**

The biggest mistake I hear about when students describe failed attempts at organizing papers are one that begin with, "First I gathered up all the boxes of papers going back to 1985." These stories have a common theme: discouragement.

As the organizer works slowly through the backlog, incoming papers keep piling up. One day he looks around only to see papers from 1985 over every surface of his office, with today's paperwork mixed in.

If you are totally out of control paper-wise, decide to start dealing with papers today. Don't go back to 1990. Don't go back to last year. Don't go back to the beginning of the year. Start with every paper that comes across your desk or through your mailbox today, and deal with it appropriately and thoroughly.

You will have to eventually wade through some of the backlog at tax time, or some other time, but for now, focus on not letting your backlog grow by a single paper.

The skills you hone will help you when it comes to dealing with the backlog and if you start keeping up with your influx of papers today, in five years you'll have half a decade of properly filed papers to work with.

A Few Suggested File Headings

Make sure you cover the basics:

Bank Statements, etc.
Car repairs
Charity
Church
Clubs (use name if justi-fied)
Correspondence
Decoration
Dining
Entertainment
Fashion
Financial
Bills to pay this month (or week)
Bills to pay next month (or week)
Files for each type of bill, e.g., phone bill, VISA bills, etc.
Health & Fitness
Insurance (Don't forget Cafeteria Plan at work)
Legal papers
Medical Information (if different from Health)
Repairmen
Schools
Taxes
Travel
Valuables
Vet
Warranties

9

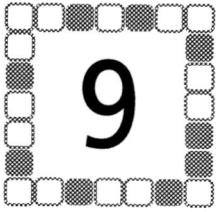

Dealing with Newspapers and Magazines

It is sometimes a painful epiphany for some folks when I tell them the truth: Magazines do not add to your net worth! There are very few magazines that ever become collectors' items. Even mint-condition *National Geographics* aren't worth very much, because there are hundreds of thousands of issues in storage all over the country. Every pack rat in the nation saves every issue.

"Collector's items" are a strange paradox when it comes to books and magazines. The more likely it is that everyone saved it, the less valuable it is. In the library I see folks all the time who bring to me a carefully wrapped edition of Shakespeare. They point to the imprint date—1898—convinced they are looking at early retirement. Unfortunately, people have a lot of respect for Shakespeare, and many people have kept volumes of his work through the decades. In the book world 1898 isn't terribly old, and in many cases, Shakespeare isn't terribly rare. Thus the carefully saved book is not worth much at all. These same, harsh principles apply to most magazines.

Let's go over some tips for dealing with magazine subscriptions. It seems as if every household has at least three or four magazine subscriptions—and some have a lot more. We're avid readers at my house, and at one time we went on a magazine "diet" and started letting subscriptions lapse. We simply had too many to keep up with.

1. Set your magazine reading priorities to focus on what's important to you

Select magazines and professional journals that will benefit you in some way—pleasure, edification, etc. If Aunt Gretna gives you Knitters Monthly every year and you don't read it, either gently tell her so, or thank her profusely and throw it away as soon as it arrives every month.

2. Make time to read the subscriptions that are important to you

Don't just skim through a magazine twelve times. Go ahead and read what interests you and get done with it. Read only the articles that pertain to you. You can rip these out for later reading, if need be. The point is to "consume " the magazine and get it out of your life. It is easy to fall into the habit of just picking through a magazine again and again. The problem is you have never "finished" with it—there's always something else you plan to look over, and so you never throw it away.

> Decide how many back issues you will keep of any one magazine, then throw away the rest.

3. Read effectively and efficiently

Take your own magazines with you when going to appointments where waiting is likely. (Waiting in the car for kids to get through with piano lessons, for example, or airports and doctor's offices.) If you pick up a magazine in a waiting room, you'll be halfway through with an article when they call you. Then you'll have to decide if you're going to steal it to finish it later. If you do steal it you'll not only feel guilty, you'll also have more clutter in your home or office.

4. Set Limits

Decide how many back issues you will keep of any one magazine. News magazines may be tossed sooner than say, Architectural Digest. Decide how many issues you'll archive and about every two months go through the house and discard all magazines that have "expired." For those you are archiving, put them in magazine files on shelves.

Setting limits in this area has brought enormous peace to my marriage. I am married to a pack rat. Specifically, he's the paper-type pack rat. When I married him I knew I was marrying a decade's worth of *Road & Track Magazine*. He keeps every issue. I knew on the front end that not only was he bringing his decade worth of *R&T*, and but also that every new issue that crosses our threshold is a permanent household addition.

Fine. We keep them all. (After all, he's a pretty great husband and I can compromise.) After *R&T*, however, we had a few conflicts about how long to keep magazines. We developed a "policy." Here it is.

If you've decided an issue was worth saving, so did a million other folks.

Road & Track—keep forever. *Kiplinger's Personal Finance Magazine*—keep two years. *US News & World Report*—keep six months. *Real Simple*—keep until read, but not longer than six months. *Fitness and Shape*—glance through, get depressed, and toss.

This approach isn't rocket science, and it keeps us from renegotiating every time I want to clear up some old magazines that clutter up the living room.

5. Special Situations with "collectors' item" magazine issues

For the few mementos you are most attached to —say the "Elvis is Dead" issue of a newspaper, get an acid-free box and box it up, along with the five other "priceless" news events you have saved, and label the box clearly. This way when your children clean out your house for the estate sale, they'll know to throw it away without even opening it.

My point is this: if you've decided an issue was worth saving, so did a million other folks. Unless you invest in deacidification and climate-controlled storage, your copy is self-destructing itself anyway. If you are utterly convinced you have this century's equivalent of a Gutenberg, consult a dealer and make sure.

6. Be realistic

Okay, so the issue you have may well be worth $10. That's retail; the most you'll ever get is wholesale, and then only if you can find a collector who is interested. How much trouble are you going to go through to get that issue to a collector? You'll probably keep it until the acid in the paper turns it to dust, at which point it will be worthless. Go ahead and get rid of it now. Or recycle it to someone with more space in his or her home or office than you have.

Then there's eBay®. I've sold books on eBay® with some success. But it is work. You have to set up your account, enter the auction, keep up with the auction—answering emails from folks who ask questions—and then pack and ship the item. I can honestly say that every eBay® transaction I have completed has been a success. My buyers paid and were pleased with their items.

But when I have considered it from a time standpoint, I am not sure I made very much money for the time and effort I put in. If you are technically savvy, like the Internet, have access to a digital camera and/or a scanner then maybe it is worthwhile. If you have a busy life with lots to do, it may not be the best way to dispose of things.

> A "Keep it for auction" refrain could become an excuse to keep things that serve your life no real or helpful purpose.

Unless you are certain an item is in demand, I'd make it a policy to not save things for auction. There is simply too high a likelihood that the "keep it for auction" refrain will become an excuse to keep things that serve your life no real or helpful purpose.

10

The Tickle File

Paula Royalty, a leading organization expert, describes pending items as the number one paper problem in America. What is a Pending Item? It is one of those items that sit on your desk while you wait for the right time to use it. You may be waiting for next Thursday's "Pizza Day" to use the pizza coupon on your desk. A pending item could be information to be discussed at next week's meeting. It is an item you need again too soon to set up a file, but not soon enough to finish with it right now.

The problem with these pending items is that they sit around, adding to your chaos while you wait for the right time to use them. By then you may have no idea where the items are, or you may have to sort through a three-inch stack to find them.

To avoid pending paper problems, you can set up a very simple system to track them until the papers are required. These systems are often called tickle files. All you'll need is an accordion pleat file.

If you happen to have one of those date sorters that lets you sort items, such as bills, by due date, then you have a tickle file. All you need to do is transfer the concept to all those random pieces of paper floating around your office. Tickle files work best in conjunction with your daily calendar.

Here's how it works.

Office supply stores sell accordion pleat files with one section for each day of the month. These files would make a suitable tickle file, as you can simply drop the item into the slot for its date. Others are available that have numbered slots, or slots for the months of the year. Think about your time frames and pick one that works for you.

For every piece of paper, you'll have to determine an action date. For many papers, the date is set, such as appointments and meetings. With these papers, you jot down all the pertinent information on your calendar or To-Do list and then file the papers in your tickle file under the date.

For example, if you have a proposal to be discussed at next month's Product Review Meeting, simply note the time, date and place of the meeting on your calendar and file in your tickle file. Make a notation on your calendar that refers to the file. If you need to peruse the proposal before the meeting, jot an additional note on your calendar a day before the meeting that refers to the proposal. Now the proposal is off your desk, but reminders have been fully documented.

To avoid pending paper problems, you can set up a very simple system to track them until the papers are required. These systems are often called tickle files. All you'll need is an accordion pleat file.

For on-going items, the key is to select a date at which you will take the next step in the process. Jot this newly created artificial deadline on your calendar, and file the item in your tickle file. Again, the paper is off your desk, but retrievable. With your calendar notations, even if someone asks you about it before the action date, a quick look at your calendar will tell you where to look.

This system works for items that tend to float around. For items for which you already have a file or folder, keep the item in its proper folder, again marking your calendar with an action date and the location of the item.

A great thing about tickle files is that other people can use them too. If you're out of the office, a tickle file makes it easy for an associate to look into a matter. You can check your calendar and say, "Under the 15th, pull those papers and fax them to me," rather than—"Look on the left-hand side of my desk—if it is not there, try the credenza—or maybe the top of the filing cabinet. It has that green logo on the corner of the cover."

11

Being More Effective at Work

Your Personal Mission Statement

In considering how to organize offices, work spaces, and other task-oriented areas, one of the first tasks is to really ask yourself, "What in the world am I doing?!?" Have you ever had an experience like the following?

You arrive at your workplace, be it the home or a remote office. You are energized and once and for all you're going to get in there and tackle that project. Today is your get it done day.

You start by realizing that unless you clear off your workspace, you'll be digging through piles of debris from previous projects and annoyances. You begin to tackle the backlog. In this case, it is filing. After about 20 minutes of filing, you come to an important memo that you'd forgotten. Since today is your "get it done" day, you decide to pause to type a brief response to the memo. You don't want that thing to stay on your desk any longer.

> **"What in the world am I doing?!?"**

After a few minutes at the computer, you realize that for the best response, you need to back up your assumptions with a little data. That's easy, and you leave the office to get the stats you need from Nancy down the hall. Nancy has the stats, but she also wants you to read over the draft of her proposal. You promise you will, and so she hands you the figures you need and a 20-page document. Again, this is your "get it done" day, and so you go straight back to your office to read the draft. That way you'll be free for the rest of the day to complete your project.

You read the draft, and in the interim get four phone calls. Three of these want information: projections on next year's production, the address of that vendor you heard about at a conference last month, and a copy of your unit's annual report from 2001 or 2003—the one with the photo of the computer in a tornado on the cover. The fourth phone call wants you to give to the United Way.

By the time you are through digging up information, including locating the copy of the annual report with the tornado on the cover, it is lunchtime. You take Nancy's draft with you to lunch and feel quite smug as you complete your critique of it.

After lunch you deliver the proposal to Nancy and return to your response to the memo. The figures Nancy provided were great, and you make several excellent points. You print off a final copy in duplicate so you have a copy for your files. This memo is a killer, and you're proud of it.

"How?" you ask yourself, "How could it possibly be worse? What in the world was I doing all day?"

Now it is nearly three p.m., time for the weekly staff meeting. You gather up your notes, sorry that you didn't have time to get prepared. But that doesn't matter; this has been your "get it done" day and your enthusiasm will make up for any lack of preparation.

After the staff meeting, you return to your office with a legal tablet full of jotted notes. Several of your notes indicate needed action. You spend a few minutes writing follow-up memos to ensure the actions will happen, including starting on the few things that are your responsibility.

By now it is almost five o'clock. You glance at your desktop, horrified. Not only is the mess worse than ever, you didn't even begin your project on your "get it done" day. All the data you needed for your memo is strewn everywhere, the filing you started, abandoned mid-stream.

"How?" you ask yourself, "How could it possibly be worse? What in the world was I doing all day?"

> Many disorganization problems occur when there is not a well-developed mission statement.

Why is it worse? Because no one kept you focused on the task you told yourself was most important. You let yourself be pulled off task repeatedly, until the day was gone. And it happens at home, too. How often have you gone to another room to get something, gotten distracted, and were almost surprised when, hours later you stumble upon the forgotten remains of your initial project? While no real live human being is ever 100% on task all the time, an effort should be made to remain focused on your highest priorities.

Your Personal Mission Statement

One of the best ways to stay on task is to develop a Personal Mission Statement. A mission statement is a conscious decision about what you are going to accomplish. If you develop a mission statement for your job, for example, you have a benchmark against which to measure every interruption and opportunity. Does this interruption add to my ability to accomplish my objective? Will this opportunity improve my productivity or effectiveness?

Many disorganization problems occur when there is not a well-developed mission for an activity. Let's think back to the "get it done" day, but this time let's apply a mission statement.

You arrive at your office and declare that today you will tackle the project that has been hanging over you for some time. That's your "Mission" for the day. First off, you clear your desk quickly—leaving stacks intact for later perusal. You know if you start to file now, you'll be drawn off task. You decide to add "file papers" to your "To-Do" list for Wednesday. The filing is off your desk, off your mind, but safely noted on your "To Do" list.

You collect the materials you need for the project. As you are gathering things up, a fellow staff member asks you for a quick opinion on a project. Looking at your watch, you say, "I can't spare the time right now, but if you'll call me this afternoon, we'll schedule a meeting."

As you begin to work on the project, you break it down into little tasks, steps, if you will. You outline the steps you want to take to complete the project. Then, remembering the purpose of the project, you decide to pare down several "would be great if" steps, and focus on only the essential, most critical elements. You know that if time permits, you can always elaborate later, but if you design a project so complex it is never finished, your career is doomed.

Small interruptions still mar your day. You answer the phone repeatedly. Each time you note the caller, the need expressed, and indicate that you are engaged right now, but will get back to the person when your calendar is clear. This technique works very well until your boss calls. He wants you to crunch some new numbers in time for the staff meeting at three. You like your job and your paycheck, so you allow this interruption. As you are crunching numbers, Boss calls back, asking for something else. You point out that you are already working on the numbers and request clarification about his priority: the new task or getting the numbers together. He chooses the numbers.

After the numbers are submitted to your boss, you see a conversation going on around the coffee urn in the break room. You are really interested, but go back to your project.

The mail truck arrives, and some really neat reading comes in…very tempting, but you decide to leave it in your in-basket until after the staff meeting, and turn your attention back to your project.

After lunch, you take a few moments to prepare for the staff meeting, and then go back to the project until time to go to the conference room. The three o'clock staff meeting pretty much kills the rest of the day, and you realize fatigue has set in.

You note how much progress you've made on the project, and resolve to pick it up again in the morning for at least two hours. In the meantime, you sort your in-basket. Those journals that looked so good when they arrived are mostly canned information you decide you don't need right now, so you toss several and file two others, unread. You scan the incoming mail, jotting notes down on each piece. Most items are immediately added to your calendar, To-Do list or Action file.

After the in-basket is cleared, you address the phone calls from earlier, checking information and phoning it back to the recipients. You feel lucky, because your office voice mail system will let you leave a message in a voice mailbox without ever speaking to the person. Thus you avoid chitchat and deliver the information you promised.

You remember your coworker who wanted your opinion on a project earlier. He hasn't called you, so you call him and offer to meet briefly either right now, or late tomorrow afternoon. He's impressed you have the time, but you know the truth. You're too tired to tackle much right now, and a brief face-to-face meeting will use the rest of your day—getting you to five o'clock and making him very happy.

After he leaves your office, you quickly review where you are with the project, making a note to yourself about where to begin in the morning. You also scan tomorrow's calendar and retrieve files you will need for several meetings. Then, just to make things more pleasant, you straighten up your desk a bit, so that in the morning, you'll find your place easily.

Your mission statement for the day has guided you all day long. It helped you stay on task, and to avoid interruptions that would have absorbed your time and energy. Yes, there were still interruptions, but you managed them more than they managed you.

Whether beginning a one-time project or starting a new job, consider the value of determining a mission statement. Some of the questions a Mission statement should answer: What am I trying to accomplish?

Some of the questions a mission statement should answer: What am I trying to accomplish? Why am I trying to make this accomplishment? Who is my audience for this accomplishment? What are the most important steps I need to address? What tools do I need to do this task? What is my deadline?

Why am I trying to make this accomplishment?
Who is my audience for this accomplishment?
What are the most important steps I need to address?
What tools do I need to do this task?
What is my deadline?

Many other questions, too, could be answered by a Mission statement, such as "What are the underlying assumptions with which I must work?" "What personal characteristics do I need to develop to do my job well?" Each mission statement will be a reflection of its author and the intent with which it was written.

12

Organization at Work

Once you have spent some time thinking about a mission statement for your work, it is time to use it to guide you in your decision-making about your workspace. Physical workplaces can be the most important element in getting a job done, after, of course, your own personal commitment to the task.

Calendars

Having (and using) a daily planner is essential to good organization. If you do not have one yet, make it a point to get one. You cannot trust your mind to hold all the details you need to remember. If you don't have a calendar yet, stop and get one—because you can't de-clutter without a way to track the essential facts on many of the papers you eliminate—and many of these facts will belong on a calendar.

What is the worst thing that could happen to me if I throw this away?
Once I put this piece of paper in its place, how will I know where to find it again?

De-Clutter

The biggest task in better organization for an office setting is to eliminate all unnecessary distractions. Distractions can be people or things — including papers, unnecessary tasks, technology and other irritants.

Using the ten principles we've used before, we need to ruthlessly weed our work spaces until they contain only those items which help us meet our mission. Clutter is your biggest enemy. When our offices (or primary work spaces—whatever their form) are cluttered, inefficiency is the natural result. When you have to move four or five other projects to clear a working space for the current project, you not only waste time, but you also increase the likelihood that you will be distracted from your primary goal and/or lose something in the shuffling process.

> De-clutter by employing the clutter removal technique described in Chapter Three. Examine each item with the principles in mind and ask, "What's the worst that could happen if I got rid of this?"

The basic cure for many distractions is to first get rid of the excess stuff in your office or workspace. Extraneous papers, varied forms of professional reading, even "award" paperweights all have one thing in common. They require your time and attention. You expend energy to maintain these items. You give them valuable space. Are all the things you keep around you helping you meet your objectives? Probably not.

I recommend that you first employ the basic de-cluttering technique to your primary workspace. For the purposes of this chapter, I will assume it is an office, but it could be a lab, a workshop, or whatever. The same principles apply.

De-clutter by employing the clutter removal technique described in Chapter Three. Set up boxes for Garbage, Give Away, Doubt, Borrowed (if needed) and Keep. (Hopefully you won't have much in the repair category—but if you are warehousing broken equipment, create that category, too.) Using the ten principles, work your way through your workspace. I'd start with something easy—like your desktop, rather than the back warehouse. Examine each item with the principles in mind and ask, "What's the worst that could happen if I got rid of this?" Don't obsess about mistakes. Just work your way through quickly.

A note on mistakes

As you may gather, I am a quick tosser. It pains my husband to no end—and sometimes I have to dispose of things discreetly so he won't ask too many questions. Over the years however, I can count only two times when I have tossed things I later regretted. And the amusing part is that I have forgotten what one of them was.

Obviously it must have caused me very little inconvenience and distress if I can't even recall the item. The thing I do remember was a dog bed. My dog forgave me.

When you decide to de-clutter your office, try to do it on a weekend, or over a long holiday weekend if you think it is a multi-day project. It is better to do this work alone, away from curious stares, when you can take the stuff to the dumpster discreetly.

One attorney who took my class de-cluttered his workspace and nearly filled a dumpster in a single weekend. Having permission to get rid of obsolete files and papers motivated him to really purge his over-filled office. He probably wouldn't have gotten as far with the phone ringing, secretaries quipping "It is about time!" or colleagues ribbing him about five large garbage bags in the hall.

Consider it a party for one, dress comfortably, play some music, if that motivates you, and go to work.

Consider it a party for one, dress comfortably, play some music, if that motivates you, and go to work.

Reduce the intake

Before acquiring anything, ask yourself how it will help you in accomplishing your mission. At a conference, exhibitors have all those nifty freebies available. Will another ruler really make you more effective? If the answer is "Yes," and you'd planned to get another ruler anyway, consider yourself fortunate and take it. Otherwise, walk away. Your office is not intended to be a warehouse! Be very critical in evaluating and retaining new items in your workspace.

If you are parking something on a bookcase, credenza or desktop only because you cannot think of another place to put it, re-think your action. Determine the best place for the item, and immediately take action to ensure it gets to its better location. Many objects end up in the way because no one took the time to really decide the best place for them. And don't forget our bonus principle: If in doubt, don't buy it or add it.

Reduce "Other Clutter"

While most of us think of clutter as "stuff," it can also be tasks. Be slower to say, "Yes," not because you are unhelpful, but because you "want to focus your energy on your top priorities." Use this line when you say, "No." Try to avoid life clutter of annoying obligations that only decrease your energy and focus.

Other clutter can also be office gossip, discussions of last night's *CSI*, or any number of other non-work-related distractions. Be mindful of these distractions and eliminate them as needed. You can't simply stop socializing with your co-workers, because human relationships are very important in getting work done. But you can be selective about the amount of time you invest in the more trivial of office activities.

> Before acquiring anything, ask yourself how it will help you in accomplishing your mission.

Beware the New Filing Cabinet Syndrome

If your filing system is effective and you always easily find information you need, then you might discover you have a real need for a new filing cabinet. Before adding one in this instance, I'd consider a serious purge of older files. By purging (use a shredder, if necessary) you may delay the purchase.

If, on the other hand, your system is a disaster with your filing cabinet crammed full and you can hardly ever find anything without a major struggle—definitely do not buy a new filing cabinet!
Instead, work on addressing your filing (or lack thereof) issues first,

purging useless paper and filing things appropriately. Adding a new filing cabinet to a chaotic filing system is just a fertile greenhouse for more chaos.

Control your reading material

Professional reading material is a problem for all of us. With so much of it to keep abreast of, we are fearful that our careers will suffer if we don't stay up to date on everything.

When I worked for a major research university, we subscribed to more than 13,000 periodicals. Can you believe that many faculty members acted frustrated because we didn't have enough? For every splintered field of specialized knowledge, there are specialized journals that address issues that matter only to the experts in those fields. With so much information out there, it is impossible to even attempt to stay on top of it all. My suggestion is that you surrender hopes of ever doing so select one or two small pieces of the information pie to focus on, and discard the rest.

> If your filing system is a disaster with your cabinet crammed full and you can hardly find anything without a major struggle—do not buy a new filing cabinet!

Focus your reading on things you need to know to be more effective. Once you choose a topic or two to focus on, you can study these issues for a few months or years, and then put them to rest and select new areas to develop. The task becomes more "do-able" and your time is better spent on issues that pertain directly to your interests than on a scatter shot of information about a hundred different topics.

In 1999, when I was faced with automating my workplace, I collected dozens of articles and special issues of magazines devoted to library automation. Once I had selected my system, I stopped reading about other systems. For one thing, the next generation is always better, and since I had jumped into the automation stream when I did, it was pointless to read about innovations in 2002 that weren't an option when I was choosing. But today, faced with selecting the next generation of automated system for my library, I am beginning to read on the topic again. My decision is months away—but I want to read as much as I can before facing the decision. Use this technique to save your valuable time.

Most of us are "as-needed" learners, anyway, which means we are most likely to successfully learn and retain new information when we need to know it. Thus, if we don't have a short-term need to know something, the likelihood is great that we won't retain the information well.

The key is to remember that there are numerous societal structures designed to collect and organize information (libraries, corporate archives and professional societies, to name a few). Let these organizations do their jobs, and let go of information that does not meet a short-term goal you have. Yes, one day you are going to master PowerPoint. But if you're swamped right now, and there is little likelihood that you will have time to learn PowerPoint for the next six months, you'll be better off not archiving that information. By the time you are ready for it, there may well be a newer version of the software available anyway.

> Most of us are "as-needed" learners, anyway, which means we are most likely to successfully learn and retain new information when we need to know it.

Prevent "Sticky Note–itis:" Make your reminders significant

Is your workspace covered with 3M sticky notes? You probably use these notes as reminders. Have you ever noted something on one of these lifesavers, but still missed the appointment or deadline? Here's why. After you have more than one or two posted, your brain learns to ignore them. Ditto with the notes on your refrigerator. If you leave little reminders around as permanent décor, they become a part of the routine static your brain has learned to filter out.

Instead of posting little pieces of papers all around, learn to note things on your calendar or your daily To-Do list. Then you'll have all your tasks in a single place, not just the ones you've jotted on sticky notes. If you almost never have sticky notes pasted all over the place, when you do have one, you will truly see it instead of just adding to the clutter in your workspace.

> Instead of posting little pieces of papers all around, learn to note things on your calendar or your daily To-Do list.

Point of use

Remember the Pareto Principle — the 80-20 Rule? Take dead files off your desk or out of the front of your filing cabinet. You might consider grouping supplies and materials on a project basis, so when you turn your attention to a different task, all the needed supplies are in a single place. I've been known to file my filing supplies—like those plastic tabs you use on hanging files—right in my filing cabinet under F for "filing supplies." I use accordion-pleated files big enough to put file folders, papers, scissors and everything I need for a project, in one easy-to-reach place. I tape a phone list of frequently called (but not enough to memorize) phone numbers right on my desk. Ugly, perhaps, but very effective.

Use Your Energy Well

I have a boss who writes scholarly books. Despite a grueling workload and responsibilities in four states, he still manages to write hefty tomes on subjects way over my head. He uses his energy well. I've noticed he seldom schedules morning meetings. I suspect that's because he uses those hours for his most demanding tasks. That's a really smart thing to so.

Do you know if you're a morning person or an afternoon person? If your brain works better on one schedule than another, try to complete your most important assignments when you're at your mental and physical best. If, for example, you know you're almost useless until 10 a.m., try to spend your morning hours doing tasks that are less challenging. Maybe this is a good time to schedule your correspondence activities, answer email and return phone calls. If you can get away with it, maybe you could schedule those boring meetings during this time.

Avoid the Internet

Okay—you can't really avoid the Internet completely, but you can take careful note of how much time you idle away surfing the web or answering chatty emails from friends. If need be, resolve to reduce your news- or weather-surfing time.

Stay on Task

Using your "Mission Statement," focus on your specified project. Resist the urge to be distracted. Keep your To-Do list handy, and continue to add to it as your mind brings items to the surface that will need your attention later. Don't start doing each of these, one by one, because you will set off a chain reaction that will absorb your entire day. As you come across material objects that need attention, say items on your desk that belong in central supplies, or files that belong to a co-worker, put all of these in a single place to deal with at once. Don't start making 18 trips all over the office to get rid of these things. Stay on task.

> Using your "Mission Statement," focus on your specified project. Resist the urge to be distracted.

Delegate

What is the WORST thing that could happen? Our famous question that applies to papers applies to many other issues in the workplace. If there is absolutely no negative consequence for not doing a task, real thought should be given to whether you should be doing it at all. If it has to be done, maybe it can be done by someone else. If at all possible and appropriate, delegate.

Delegation can be tricky for some people, because they like to hang onto authority. Learn to give away responsibility when it is appropriate. In certain cases, delegation only makes good business sense. To be fair, when you delegate a task, you should also grant the authority to get it done. Nothing is more frustrating for a subordinate than to have a responsibility without authority. For example, we've all run into a professional, pleasant customer service representative who could empathize with our problem, but who could not solve it. That situation aggravates everyone involved.

Before delegating a task, ask yourself a variation of the question we've used repeatedly, "What's the worst thing that will happen if this is never done?" If the answer is "nothing," consider letting the task go. Employees are quick to see busy work; if it is busy work, that means there is real work going un-addressed.

Delegate to other's strengths. If you know your subordinate's strong points, you can delegate tasks that reinforce these strengths. If you know Mary is a terrible public speaker, but Jim enjoys it, send Jim to make the presentation. Yes, as a

> **If a task doesn't move you closer to your Mission, it is probably delaying you in getting there.**

supervisor you must "grow" and "stretch" your subordinates, but choose the occasions to do so where the payoff is greatest and the risk least.

Delegate with specifics. Assign a task with a built-in accountability structure. Every assignment should have a due date as well as clearly articulated expectations. Unclear assignments result in unclear products. While you outline due dates and expected outcomes, it is best to allow the person a choice in exactly how to meet the deadline and objective. If you spend as much energy delegating in minute detail as you would in completing the task (or worse—redoing the task) you have either a control problem or a subordinate problem.

Delegate with real deadlines. Never simply say "A.S.A.P." When you tell someone you need something "as soon as possible" you really aren't saying much at all. Instead, give a specific time. "I need this by 1 o'clock so that I can review it before I meet with Jim." ASAP might mean, "when you get around to it."

Get to work on time

It may be a no-brainer, but one of the biggest things you can do to be more organized at work is to get there on time and well rested. Staying up late the night before and dragging yourself out of bed—late again—is almost guaranteed to add a layer of stress to your day. When you start off feeling behind, you are more stressed, more frantic, and more likely to let things slide into disorganization. You're late to work and there's a meeting first thing. You dash into your cubicle, throwing down everything on top of whatever is already there. When you get back from the meeting, your voice mail is already full and you are nervous because it is almost lunchtime and some of those messages may be from eight o'clock this morning. You hope none of them is from your boss.

> Never simply say "A.S.A.P." When you tell someone you need something "as soon as possible" you really aren't saying much at all.

This scenario is a model for a stressful day. Getting to work on time won't relieve you of your responsibilities, but it will allow you to be more peaceful as you tackle your day. Another benefit is this: it removes lingering guilt you have over not getting enough done. If you put in your full workday—and then maybe a bit more—you can leave your office with a clear conscience.

13

Technology

Don't let technology manage you!

With the technology that surrounds us today, it is easy to let technology set our agenda. Technology should be our tool, not a driving force for our days. How often do you interrupt a conversation with a real live, present person to answer a phone call that may be from a telemarketer?

We often elevate technology to the level of a taskmaster instead of a helper.

How many of you are slaves to email? Is it difficult to not check your email every hour or so? How many of you interrupt almost any activity, including sleep, when a telephone rings? It is easy to let technology take over.

> We often elevate technology to the level of a taskmaster instead of a helper.

Here are some concrete ways to deal with common technology-based problems. Before considering these, remember that the ten principles apply here, too. A simple decision to not react to every incoming email message can be a big relief. You can realize that membership on a list-serve is only marginally useful and have your name removed from the list.

Email

If your computer gives an audible chime every time an email message comes in, you are acutely aware of every new message. How much time do you spend transitioning from your current activity to the email server program? If it is only a few minutes each time, over the course of the day that could add up to an hour. Try to address your email load only once or twice each day. Dealing with several email messages at once will help you to ration your time. When you see 16 messages needing a response, you'll be less likely to spend too much time on a single reply.

Ask yourself if a reply email message is really the best response. Maybe something old fashioned—such as the telephone, would be more helpful. This choice is especially true in cases where you are negotiating things. Rather than jockey back and forth six times in setting up a meeting, call the person and ask them to open their calendar and look at theirs while you look at yours.

> Is an email really the best response? Maybe something old fashioned—such as the telephone, would be more helpful.

Virtually all email programs have "folders" where you can archive items by sender or topic. If you find yourself hanging onto email messages (and you are absolutely certain this is essential and not just an electronic form of clutter) be sure to file them, rather than leaving them in one big pile in your electronic in-basket.

Telephone Management

Do you manage your phone, or does it manage you? Do you pick up every phone call all the time, or do you schedule blocks of time where you let your phone roll over to voice mail, thus allowing yourself a period of concentrated work? The days of secretaries and assistants are nearly behind us, with fewer and fewer white-collar workers enjoying the presence of these saints. Now most of us answer our own phones and do our own word processing. Thus, it falls to us to manage our own phones rather than having our assistant screen calls for us.

When blocks of time are needed, use your phone as a tool. Let it take messages during your period of concentrated work.

On your outgoing voice mail greeting consider recording commonly requested information. Your fax number or email address, for example, or hours of operation, if appropriate. Also, instruct callers to leave information that is helpful. Do you want a brief message, or a detailed recitation of the caller's issue?

> When calling someone, a few pre-emptive moves will make your time a better investment. Jot down a list of issues that you hope to address in the call. Announce up front how many items you need to address.

When calling someone else, a few pre-emptive moves will make your time a better investment. For starters, jot down a list of issues that you hope to address in the call. Announce up front how many items you need to address. "Jim, I need your input on two things about the Fielding project." This approach will keep you on task and also serve as a guide of what to mention if you wind up leaving a message. When you do reach voice mail, be sure to clearly identify yourself. Don't just say, "This is Barney." He may not know your last name or what department you work for. Again, indicate how many items you are addressing, so the person you are calling doesn't delete your message after the first request. Leave your phone number every time you call. On a hectic day, a ready phone number may make the difference between a returned call and one ignored. I know it does for me.

A Radical Idea

What if you simply decided to not have an answering machine or voice mailbox? Think about the consequences. If you were away from your phone and a caller could not leave a message, that caller would call back, perhaps again and again, until he or she reached you. With an answering machine, the caller leaves a message, obligating you to take action: do something, return the call or whatever.

Until a message lands on your voice mail, you do not have any obligation to take any action. Thus, if a caller leaves a long detailed message about wanting you to play for the company softball team, you have to call back and say "No." If you didn't have a machine to take the message, you'd be free of that obligation.

> **Until a message lands in your voice mail, you do not have any obligation to take any action.**

I know this may be impossible in a work situation, but it may be a viable option for home application. Life without an answering machine or voice mail might be simpler in the long run.

14

Time Management

Everyone has heard the old, worn-out saying, "Everyone has the same amount of time in a day—24 hours!" I don't know who first said it, but I suspect it was someone who had very few responsibilities. Yes, we all have 24 hours. But some of us have a lot more responsibilities than others. Admitting this difference is important. We shouldn't beat ourselves up when we seem to be forever behind. Instead, a better way to spend precious energy is to try to manage time well, eliminate anything that can be safely eliminated from our lives, and to set priorities.

> We all have 24 hours in a day. But some of us have a lot more responsibilities than others!

Make time; don't wait for it

This concept applies to big dreams (becoming a screenwriter) and small chores (vacuuming the living room). If you wait until you have time, you probably won't accomplish your dream. If it is a chore, you'll do it at the last possible minute, do it poorly, and resent your efforts and the result. Make time.

Take advantage of the mini-blocks of time in your life

(Remember the "One more thing" rule?) If you find yourself with 12 minutes to spare, draft a memo about the parking problem. If you see you have five minutes before you have to leave for work, start the dishwasher or a load of laundry — the washer, not the dryer, unless the load is immune to wrinkles. If you have 15 minutes, you can't tackle a whole project, but you can make a list of action steps and number them in priority order. You can return a phone call, address an envelope, and purge some files from your desk.

Pare down

Ask yourself what you can jettison in your life. Can you resign from a committee you hate? Can you eliminate your answering machine, thereby relieving yourself of having to return phone calls? (It leaves the ball in the caller's court.) Can you decide to never again buy Dry Clean Only clothes? Decide not to do the things that have been on your To-Do list for more than a month, or a year, whatever time frame makes you realize it is not a critical item. If you're not going to do something, admit it, accept responsibility and move on. My dog has bad teeth and the vet recommends daily brushing. I honestly tried, but spending 20 minutes every evening wrestling with my already-neurotic dog was simply miserable. So I gave up. I now pay to have her teeth professionally cleaned twice a year. It costs more than human teeth cleaning! But I am willing to pay that price to avoid daily aggravation.

> Spend some time each week planning the entire week—not just your day.

Plan ahead

Spend some time each week planning the entire week—not just your day. What are the major accomplishments you need to see this week? Schedule them day by day. Include your personal tasks, too. Use your calendar and note on each day the things you need to accomplish that day.

Quantify your time's value

To help in justifying new activities or the elimination of old activities, calculate the value of your time. How much is an hour of your day worth? If you look at activities based on this value, are you willing to invest that amount in each activity?

Think realistically

In setting priorities and ranking your tasks to accomplish, figure in their complexity. Are you waiting for input from six other people? That factor may cause a dramatic increase the time required for this task— thus making it merit a longer span of time in your schedule.

Measure time

If you feel like you are spinning your wheels, conduct a time inventory for a day or two. On a sheet of paper, jot down the time you turn your attention to a task, along with a one- or two-word description of the task. Each time you change tasks, note the time and the new activity. This tool will help you see the structure (or lack thereof) of a day in your life. It may also help you identify time-wasters (an open door by the office lounge) and eliminate them or at least mitigate them.

Mark essential blocks of time on your calendar—for planning, resting, housekeeping, etc. Give yourself the same priority as you would someone else.

Think negatively

To set priorities when you just can't identify the greater importance of any one of a number of equally important tasks, try considering the negative consequences of not accomplishing each one. The one with the greatest negative impact may then become your top priority. Consider here the life-style negative impact — such as daily aggravation, as well as the threat of being fired.

Be focused

In directing a project, develop a mission statement. Determine what it is you are trying to accomplish, and then do only those things that move you toward the completion of the project your mission statement describes.

Break the action-block

Do the hardest (or yuckiest) part of a task first. That way your dread won't stop you from proceeding.

Write it down

Keep lists of tasks, things to buy, measurements for things you need. Then, when you have that extra mini-block of time, you can glance at your list and decide what to tackle next.

Schedule yourself

Mark essential blocks of time on your calendar—for planning, resting, housekeeping, etc. Give yourself the same priority as you would someone else.

Keep a master list and master calendar

Somewhere in your life you need to track all of your obligations in a single place. This is your master list. Also write these items on your family's master calendar. Your master calendar should indicate obligations at least a year into the future. Mark planned vacation days, projects, seasonal chores and other easily forgotten things. If you consult a master calendar before taking on new commitments, you won't find yourself accepting an obligation, only to remember, weeks later, that it conflicts with your planned vacation—or worse—occurs on top of another huge project, guaranteeing you severe stress and frustration for weeks. (More on the master list coming up.)

15

Procrastination

We all procrastinate at some point in our lives. It is human nature to put things off. It is possible, however, to procrastinate to the point where it interferes with our lives. Human nature, maybe, but we've got to find a way past the action-block.

You've heard of writer's block, haven't you? That inexplicable malady that causes words and thoughts to vanish when faced with an empty page? That's closely akin to action-block.

You have action-block when you know you need to do something. You have to do it. There's no getting around it. It has to be done. But you don't do it. Instead you avoid it. Pretend it isn't there. Distract yourself with other, more attractive activities.

> It is human nature to put things off.

This form of procrastination leads to action-block, which in turn seems to manifest itself in the back of your mind as dread. I've dreaded things so much and so long that when I finally got around to doing them, it was a relief. In fact, I've spent more time and energy dreading a task then the task itself takes. Boy. What a waste!

Before we start discussing action-block busters we need to really address all sides of procrastination. Sure, it causes undue dread, sleepless nights and may be even stress-induced heartburn. But you know what? It sometimes works!

In my career as a librarian, I've seen procrastination in all its forms. One especially upsetting version includes the over-involved parent, the scenario when I see a parent actually doing their child's research.

Tah-dah! The child's procrastination worked big time. He didn't want to do the research, put it off, and out of the blue a rescuer (frequently mom or a girlfriend) saves the day. The sad truth is, sometimes procrastination pays off.

On some tasks, if you procrastinate long enough, the need to complete the task just fades away. Put off doing the paperwork for a rebate and the rebate's void. Manufacturers actually count on folks doing this. Graduate school? The long and tedious application process must be complete by March 1st; delay long enough and there won't be enough time to get the paperwork done. A side benefit here is you don't have to deal with possible rejection if you "don't have enough time" to apply.

This leads us to another way procrastination pays off: If you do everything at the last minute, you can always blame lack of time for a sub-par or mediocre job. It is not you, you tell yourself. You're not really a "C" student; you just didn't give yourself enough time to write the "A" paper you know you are capable of. Having an explanation (lack of time) is useful to a lot of people.

> On some tasks, if you procrastinate long enough, the need to complete the task just fades away.

Despite the few ways procrastination "works," though, it has far more negative consequences than positive ones. From late fees to friendly little chats with the IRS, procrastination can keep you in hot water with a lot of people—from your spouse to your boss. It is not a peaceful way to live.

Let's talk ourselves out of this bad habit. First, drop the myth that you work better under pressure. Students who start their research projects sooner make far better grades than those who wait till the last minute. "But that's not a fair comparison. You're comparing an A project that took three weeks to a C project that took three hours!" complained one of my students.

Using your own "I do better under pressure" argument, that C paper would have been a D or F if started three weeks earlier. You don't really believe that do you?

> **Procrastinators invite more stress into their lives.**

The truth is when we are under pressure, stressed out and tired, we don't perform our best. Adrenaline can take the human mind and body only so far. And if you live on a perpetual diet of adrenaline, you probably become somewhat dulled to its performance-boosting properties.

To further beat the "better under pressure" myth into the ground, consider this fact. College students who procrastinate report much higher levels of stress and are more likely to develop colds and other illnesses by the time finals roll around. Ever attempted a calculus final with a fever and runny nose? I'll bet it is not a pretty sight.

Procrastinators simply invite more stress into their lives. They invite guilt over things not done, gifts never purchased, letters never written. It does not make for a peaceful existence.

Action-block busters
Here are some strategies to help you break through procrastination. Use them in combination with one another.

Break down the task you are procrastinating on into steps. If it is a large project, your steps may be broken down even further. Don't do this task in your mind. Do it on paper. Spend some time listing all the steps, no matter how mundane.

Trick yourself into starting the task. There's an expression we use in my part of the country. It is "I'm fixing to" do something. Note that the speaker isn't actually indicating a start to the task; rather he or she is indicating a willingness to prepare to do the task. "I'm fixing to go to prayer meeting" may involve a change of clothes, a shower or whipping up a dessert to take along. When someone is fixing to get ready to go, you don't go crank up the car. You might be an hour away from leaving.

How does this help cure action-block? Easy—it sets the stage and helps reveal how simple the task is.

> "I'm fixing to go to prayer meeting" may involve a change of clothes, a shower or whipping up a dessert to take along.

If you are fixing to get ready to write a report you might do these things-
- Get some paper
- Boot up your computer
- Gather your notes
- Pull together your information
- Gather some additional information
- Brew some coffee

When you've done all these things, no one's said you have to start writing. You're just "fixed" to go. But, once all these things are done, it is far easier to start the project. You don't have to start it—just put your list of steps on top of the note pad you've lain out—or lean it up against the monitor. You may even discover you've done some of the steps.

And if you've started completing the steps, you're not procrastinating anymore.

If dreading a task is sapping your energy, try breaking the task into steps and evaluating each step. Which ones do you really dread?

Figure this out and get those out of the way first. You may find your desire to procrastinate is gone, once you've eliminated the parts that you liked least or dreaded most. I love having parties. But the task I dread the most—addressing the invitations-- can really stop me in my tracks. If I can make myself sit down and address them—every one—even the ones where I have to look up the zip code—then everything else is a piece of cake. Polishing silver, no big deal. Cleaning up, not a problem. Everything is easier once I've finished the task I like the least.

And it is important I do all of it—all the way to locating missing zip codes. If I do everything but "the hard ones" the task still hangs in the back of my mind nagging me.

What about delegating a dreaded task? If you've procrastinated on the same type of task—say arranging committee meetings—maybe there's someone else in your organization (or household) who could do it better.

> Some tasks you procrastinate can simply be deleted from your "to do" list. Just be prepared to accept consequences gracefully.

You could always pay someone to do the things you put off. Hate tax forms? Find an accountant. Gutters haven't been cleaned out in, oh, forever? Hire someone to do it.

Some tasks you procrastinate on can simply be deleted from your "to do" list. Just be prepared to accept the consequences gracefully. If you decide to give up on the gutters and leave them clogged with debris year round, put aside some money for repair bills. Or spend money now on high-quality gutter guards so you don't have to worry about it.

You might want to bargain with yourself. If you accomplish the dreaded task, you'll celebrate by doing something you wouldn't otherwise. Rewards tend to work better than punishments. We can tell ourselves, "If I don't pay bills tonight, I won't watch *CSI*." But often we procrastinate and watch the TV show anyway. So think of a reward that's really a reward. It is important that it be something you wouldn't do otherwise, or you'll just procrastinate and buy yourself the DVD anyway.

Gather witnesses! Tell other people that you are about to attack the dreaded task. Better yet, ask them to hold you accountable. I've told my co-workers "I've got a deadline. If you see me outside my office for more than a rest room break—send me back to work." This technique can be really effective.

> "I'm procrastinating less and less every day. I'm getting better about not putting things off."

Schedule time for the task—officially—in your date book. By blocking out time you address one of your biggest excuses: No time.

Just do it. Nike says it best. Stop talking, thinking about it, agonizing over it, dreading it, complaining about it—just do it. The mere act of starting may be what it takes to break through your action-block.

Keep it up. If you've been a lifelong, severe procrastinator, you are not likely to break the habit in a day or two. Tell yourself "I am going to stop procrastinating," and then, task-by-task, work through the bad habit. It is probably not helpful to say, "I'll never, ever procrastinate again" when you know that future procrastination is likely. That's setting yourself up for failure and gives legs to defeatist self-talk. "There, I've procrastinated again—I'm doomed. I'll never get out of this." That kind of "all-or-nothing" thinking is a hindrance to overcoming procrastination. Instead, tell yourself "I'm procrastinating less and less every day. I'm getting better about not putting things off."

Before long, you'll be living proof that action-block does not have to be a chronic malady.

16

Organization on Autopilot

The best forms of organization are those that lead to consistently and painlessly accomplishing a routine task. Some tasks lend themselves to "automatic" organization. You need to set up a method (or system) of accomplishing these tasks and then employ the method until it becomes a habit.

How do you get tasks to work easily?

1. Keep it simple. If you make it too complicated, it won't work. I have simple "systems" for dealing with certain items around the house. Everything to do with "light" is in a certain cupboard—flashlights, candles, matches, spare batteries, and even extra light bulbs are all kept in one place. I never have to think about where I might have stashed spare bulbs or a flashlight. A grocery list is stuck to the fridge at all times. If I were to conceal it in a pretty basket or inside a cupboard, we'd seldom use it.

Here are some tasks that lend themselves to "automatic" organization

■ Paying bills
■ Keeping a Family Master Calendar that logs each member's activities
■ Keeping a personal calendar
■ Keeping an address book
■ Sorting incoming mail
■ Processing email
■ Handling voice mail

2. Make it consistent. Keeping like things together, for instance, is logical and systematic. I keep all our vases on one shelf in our laundry room. I never have to wonder where a vase is. It is either out on display or on this shelf.

3. Employ the Point of Use principle. Consider placing items needed as you leave the house near the door, for example. We have a large, ugly heavy-duty coat rack right by the door. This is where I hang dog leashes, umbrellas, hats and coats. When I have to make sure I take an item to work, I often put it in a handle bag and hang it on this rack. Even when I don't need to wear a coat, I can still see the bag in plain view.

It is best to try to keep frequently used items "one reach" away. If you use certain kitchen tools when at the stove, consider keeping them in a jar or crock right on the stove top or counter. That way you don't have to reach once to open a drawer, a second time to get the needed implement and a third time to close the drawer. In the kitchen, items used daily are in the lower overhead cabinets. In the laundry room, I leave the box of soap out in plain view. We consume a lot of rice, so it is kept in a canister on the kitchen counter, even though we know that most people use the largest canister in a set for sugar or flour.

4. Group things in a single location. I keep envelopes, return address labels and stamps all in one place. I keep all my "morning" vitamins and medicines in the kitchen, where I eat my breakfast, and my "evening" supplements in the bathroom drawer. I am much more likely to actually take my vitamins this way. At work, I have a worktable in my office upon which I keep scissors, tape, paper clips, a stapler, pens and pencils, as well as some 3M sticky notes. These materials are actually duplicates of items I keep in my desk drawer, but when I use the table for meetings or to spread out a project, it is very convenient to have everything I need at hand.

> It is best to try to keep frequently used items "one reach" away.

For other types of projects, I use large file folders with accordion pleated sides. The trick is that I not only keep the papers I'm working on here, but also three-dimensional objects that will fit as well. I might stuff in markers and name tag badges along with handouts to take to a meeting or class. I might put a stack of papers, a book or two, and a pad of 3M™ sticky notes to use for jotting down ideas as I review a manuscript or article. I've even been known to slip a small bottle of aspirin into a file, when I'm taking it to a taxing meeting. The point is, I am able to "bunch" things by topic, and not have to scrounge around for needed items every time I turn to a project.

5. Create coding systems. I keep all files relating to money in green files. Household files are blue. With laundry, it is helpful to code kids' clothes. One system I know of dealt with the issue of hand-me-downs very well. The oldest son had no markings on his clothes. When an item became outgrown and was passed on the second son, a single black dot was added in an inconspicuous place. In the cases where the item lasted until the third son could use it, a second dot was added to the first. These dots were also used on new clothes purchased for the boys.

> The key to using systems to make your life easier is to keep them simple. The best system in the world, if it is too complicated to implement, isn't very useful at all.

The key to using systems to make your life easier is to keep them simple. The best system in the world, if it is too complicated to implement, isn't very useful at all. In our coding example, if the mother of the boys decided to buy cute embroidered labels with each of the boys' names on them she'd have to first order them, then apply them with a sewing machine, and finally change them when the item got bumped down a son. A system that is that time consuming is likely to fall by the wayside when life gets busy.

17

Our Closets: The Shame of Plenty

To show how the principles or organization apply to household areas, let's apply the principles to something we all have (and most of us dread): our closets. Closets are a good starting point because everybody has one, and most likely, it is the source of at least some dissatisfaction. If you haven't already conquered your closet, let's tackle it this week.

Do you often peer into your closet, but find little to wear? While your problem may be a legitimate shopping issue (you don't have enough clothes), it is a hundred times more likely to be an organization and thinking problem. It is an organization problem because you use your closet inefficiently. It is a thinking problem because your attitude about clothes may need adjustment.

Closets are a good starting point. Everybody has one, and it is likely the source of at least some dissatisfaction. If you haven't already conquered your closet, let's tackle it this week.

As always, the beginning step is to critically examine the contents of your closet and discard the items that are simply unnecessary. Use our principles:

If in doubt, throw it out

If you're unsure about an item, toss it. A test for this decision is hesitation. The real "keepers" are instantly obvious. When you have to use your imagination to think of when you might wear something again, odds are it is a toss item. Plan to go through your closet and evaluate every item.

Use it or lose it

If you haven't worn it in over a year, consider letting it go. If you're like most of us—by the time an event comes around to wear it to the style will be out, or your waist will be out!

Recycle

Is there a better person or place for this item? Goodwill maybe? Can this item be altered to be more stylish? Or is it fit only to be turned into a rag? Will you take the trouble to see that it happens?

Set limits

How many navy sports coats does one person need? Ditto for white shirts. Even the basics like "the classic black dress" can be overdone if the owner has an entire collection. For true basics, consider a limit—such as one short black skirt and one long black skirt.

> Set limits. For true basics, consider a limit—such as one short black skirt and one long black skirt.

One more thing

When you take something out of your closet or return it to the closet, take the time to do it right. Return hangers to an appropriate place. When re-hanging clothes, insure they are wearable for the next use. Check for soiling and possible mending needs. To make your life even easier, when tossing things into the hamper, go ahead and unbutton those tiny button-down collar buttons. Check the pockets for forgotten items. (Washed and dried lip balm can be deadly to clothes.)

A place for everything

When arranging your closet, keep like items together. Keep all jackets in one section, all slacks in another. All button-down shirts together. (I sort mine by color.) I even go as far as to have all my sleeveless shirts together, all my short-sleeved items together, etc.

Don't collect junk

If your closets are bulging, be a snob. Keep only the items that are well made and flatter you. If you feel yucky every time you wear an ensemble, by all means, send it on to Goodwill.

A Good Defense Is Proactive Shopping: Our Bonus Principle

When you shop for clothes, become highly proactive. Consider these questions before you add a new item to your closet:

Is this machine washable? If you rarely go to the dry cleaners, the item will wind up soiled and stored for weeks in a heap waiting for you to get around to having it cleaned. I've had students report outfits going out of style in the time it took to get around to dry-cleaning them.

Does this fit my lifestyle? Is it an item that you will wear repeatedly? Even for "special events" clothes, try to get versatile items. For example, if you're in the market for a classic black cocktail dress, think in terms of one that will also serve as funeral attire. If you get the ultra slinky dress that's only for parties, you'll still need another dark dress for the more somber events. Consider an in-between dress that can be made festive with accessories or toned down.

> If you feel yucky every time you wear an ensemble, by all means, send it on to Goodwill.

Will I need to alter this item? If you have a poor track record for actually getting alterations done, keep shopping.

How much will this cost per use? This question is a way of considering clothing purchases that will foster the purchase of high-quality, high-use items. For example, if you are considering a basic black belt, and you know you will wear it several times a week for several years, you can then justify spending more for higher quality leather. On the other hand, if the item has a trendy look that you suspect may not be so trendy in a year, you would want to pay less for it since it will probably have fewer wearings.

Remember, no matter how good the sale, it is money wasted if you never wear the item.

Transitional and Special Occasion Clothing Storage Tips

Swap your clothing as the seasons change. Have you ever gone a full year without really swapping your clothes? You just keep going back to the spare closet to take out one more outfit. After about ten months, your "active" closet is crammed, and your spare closet has only things you can no longer wear, or wouldn't be caught dead in. Each spring, put away your winter clothes and bring out your warm weather wardrobe. Swap them out

> No matter how good the sale, it is money wasted if you never wear the item.

in the fall. Okay, we know you'll have to leave out some outfits for those strangely cool or warm days, but put away the bulk of your one-season clothes. If you find you went all winter without wearing some of the winter clothes, it sounds like a Goodwill donation to me.

When switching your wardrobe, inventory your clothes. Thinking about the proactive shopping tips, critically decide which (if any) of the "Goodwill" candidates need to be replaced. Are your favorite items showing wear and in need of replacement? If you shop proactively and only for specific needed items, it may take a while to find the exact item you need to replace.

It is also very important to ensure the clothes you store are absolutely clean and ready for storage. Have you ever found money in the pocket of an item you took out of storage? I once stored a white linen dress with a colored paper napkin in the pocket. When I took it out the next spring, the color of the napkin had transferred itself to the dress, ruining it. Even if clothes look clean, colorless "stains" can darken over time. If in doubt, re-clean an item, if you're positive you'll want to keep it.

18

Home Organization and Our Ten Principles

Household Organization

First off, it is going to be work. The "workless house" is about as likely to arrive as the "paperless" office. Better organization will reduce your household workload, but will not eliminate it.

The first step in household organization: de–cluttering

Before organizing an area, first purge the area. Remember, my favorite principle of organization: If in doubt, throw it out. If you begin to organize before you've eliminated the excess inventory, you'll waste precious energy rearranging items that really belong in the Goodwill bin.

Remove clutter first and then organize. Ask yourself: Why am I reorganizing Mason Jars and lids when I haven't canned in 30 years and don't even have so much as a tomato plant in my yard?

Here are some concrete tips based on the ten principles that will help make your household more manageable.

Make daily pick–up a routine

Thinking of the "One More Thing" principle, go ahead and spend 15 to 20 minutes doing a quick walk-through of your home, collecting old newspapers, stray dishes, and odd shoes and socks that get dispersed everywhere. If you do this once for each room daily, your house will always be moderately presentable. It won't be dusted, but you'll have a place to sit, should company drop in.

Make this a routine you perform each day, and you'll never find yourself buried under three weeks' debris. If you have de-cluttered each room, it will be easier to keep things in their places.

A place for everything: even parking places

Create "parking places" in each room for things that don't really belong permanently in that room, but that you are using there for the time being. I wind up with small stacks of books in the den, baskets into which I toss magazines we're still reading, and so on. By limiting the space devoted to these items, they never take over, and if I want to read the current issue of Southern Living, I know it is in the stack in the basket. By using attractive parking spaces—baskets, decorative boxes, and even space on shelves, these items can be kept at hand without adding clutter to a room.

Don't collect junk

Keep a critical eye on what you add to your surroundings. Imagine a visitor walking through your front door into your living room. What would you like the visitor to know about you by what is seen? That you love books or penguins? Do you want the image presented to be calming and soothing or energetic and fun loving? Decide these things about each room in your home, and de-clutter as appropriate.

Special Note to those of us who want a maid for Christmas: If you use a house cleaning service, you will find that the greater your household organization, the more effective your housekeepers can be. If you are paying by the hour for someone to round up discarded newspapers from all over the house, you are paying top dollar for a no-brainer task that you can do in minutes on a daily basis. If you do this task yourself, your home will look neater at all times—not just the afternoon after the housekeeper comes, and your cleaning service will have more time to devote to those really icky jobs, like bathroom grout and dusty baseboards

A big issue at this point is the reality of living in your home. If you have two separate living areas, perhaps you can justify snow-white carpet and upholstered furniture in the formal living room. But if you really have to use these items, purchase colors and materials that suit your life style. If you're going to be a nervous wreck every time you have company for fear someone will spill something on your beautiful rug, you'll soon stop entertaining. Maybe you need a different rug.

The most beautiful things in the world, if they are simply not functional, just become another category of high-class junk. Let's call it junque. It still may not belong in your life.

Set limits

If the number one cause of disorganization is postponed decisions, a close second is just too much stuff. We have too much stuff in our closets, drawers, pantries, and cupboards. We can't find the things we need, so we assume we're out, go buy more, only to discover later that we already had the item hidden behind 14 other things. Set limits. No one says you can't keep some paper bags on hand. But there should be a very real limit on the number you keep. (Keep only the amount that fits into a single paper bag.)

> The most beautiful things in the world, if they are simply not functional, just become another category of high-class junk. Let's call it junque.

Remember the point of use principle

I keep Windex™ in my bathroom closet because that's what I use on the bathroom mirror. I also keep it in the kitchen because I use it on the counters and also on the floor in the event of minor spills. Try to keep household items where you need them. Everything to do with laundry should be stored in the laundry room.

Determine a place for everything

For some items, you'll need to pick a single location where they will be kept. It may not be ideal—but it needs to be definite. I keep all our light bulbs in a drawer in the dining room. Not logical, but it is consistent—all light bulbs are there—even the little tiny ones that go in the night lights.

In our kitchen we have two spaces where we keep spices. Baking spices (used rarely) are in one place, while the regular cooking spices are one reach away from the stove top. I keep party supplies way up high on the top shelf of a cabinet. I have to get a ladder to get them down. No big deal—we don't have parties every day—but I keep all that stuff together.

Having pre-approved placement for almost everything in the house is very helpful. And my placement is not super-specific. I keep "party supplies" in a single location—that's every thing from snazzy napkins to serving trays. I don't have to think of separate places for platters, party paper products, and chafing pans.

Bonus principle: If in doubt, don't buy it

Buy the simplest appliance to meet the most of your needs. If you really think you are going to heat up frozen pizza more than once or twice a month, maybe, just maybe, the pizza zapper is right for you. But I sort of doubt it. In most cases the oven works fine. Do you need a vegetable steamer, when a saucepan will do the same thing and take up less space? You can use the saucepan all the time. An electric steamer you use only to steam; the other 322 days of the year when you do not steam vegetables, the steamer is sitting there, in the way, consuming space.

Marketers today are really good at combining items to invent new products. But I'd think twice before buying a complicated combination appliance when a simpler one will do. The simpler one is easier to operate and probably has fewer parts to lose or break.

If you are on the verge of buying a new appliance or gadget, ask yourself how often you will use it versus the space, time and energy it will take up. While I have an electric can opener (a gift from my parents) we almost never use it because my 1930s kitchen counter space is very scarce. I hate to devote almost a square foot to an electric can opener when I can keep a hand model in a drawer, one reach away. The big electric can opener is kept under the sink for when I have a large number of cans to open—say, when making a huge batch of red beans and rice. I still use it, but not enough to justify giving it top value space.

Closed storage often looks better than open storage in real life

Beautiful glass front cabinets are lovely in the glossy decorating magazines that barrage us from grocery store checkout lines. But the truth is, unless you are very disciplined about putting things away very neatly every time, it may not look so great in your home. I do have some glass front cupboards in my kitchen. Luckily, I have monochrome dishes (all edges are white) and a collection of clear glassware for my everyday use. I do have a small collection of Mexican blown glass on display here too, and the light green adds visual interest. But believe me, anything I even think of adding to this cabinet is either clear or white. If I went to cheerful colors, I'd have to keep it a whole lot neater. As it is, the simple color palette makes up for a lot.

> By limiting colors, rooms appear less cluttered and more spacious. The fewer colors to clamor for your eye's attention, the more serene a space appears.

Use colors to create calm

Most of us don't think of color as an organizing tool, unless it is associated with a coding schedule. But color can be used to greatly enhance your organization. Here are some easy ways. At home, I have limited our linen colors. We have only white and sage bathroom towels. The white towels go in the guest bath, and the sage ones in the master bath. The color alone provides the "sort" key. And the look of a monochrome closet is especially pleasing to the eye. Any closet with a single color or narrow color palette looks neater than a closet with a riot of colors. Notice in upscale catalogues that show home and closet organizers that most of the clothes are neutral colors, and very few colors at that.

Besides bath towels, I've applied this color-organization principle to other linens throughout the house. Kitchen towels are purple. Master bed sheets are ecru. The powder room hand towels are multi-colored. All linens are stored in the room where they are used. Thus a stray hand towel can be easily spotted and returned to its home.

I use these same limits on colors when purchasing household supplies. All paper towels are plain white, as is facial tissue (in green boxes, if possible). By limiting colors present, rooms appear less cluttered and more spacious. I have even been known to select shampoo because I liked the color of the bottle. Sounds extreme, but the fewer colors to clamor for your eye's attention, the more serene a space appears.

19

The "Joy" of Housework

Very few people look forward to housecleaning. In spite of this aversion some housekeeping does need to get done for your home to be presentable and comfortable (especially when your parents, in-laws or boss are visiting). And while we're talking about it, why only get your house in order when company's coming? Why not enjoy a peaceful, organized home yourself? Here are some ideas about how to keep housework from taking over your life.

First, de-clutter. This step may take awhile, but the payoff justifies the work. Beside, de-cluttering your home may in itself make your home look cleaner.

If you jump into organizing, you'll just be organizing stuff you won't keep. If you try to clean first, you'll spend a lot of energy cleaning things you will later remove.

De-cluttering a home (use the directions in chapter three) is a big task and not one that should be attempted unless there is a block of time sufficient to do some good. When you work at de-cluttering your home, start small. Pick a linen closet. You want something definite, with clear boundaries, that is manageable for the time you have to devote to it. If you have three days, tackle the garage. If you have 30 minutes, do the junk drawer in the kitchen.

Once you have de-cluttered, you are ready to organize. You may be tempted to jump straight into cleaning, but with the exception of perhaps wiping down a shelf before you return its rightful contents, don't.

What's the difference between cleaning and organizing? Organization happens to look a lot like cleaning—and the results appear to be similar—a neater, more presentable area.

The difference is the underlying issue. The issue with cleaning is dirt—a physical manifestation of "yuck." The underlying issue with disorganization is mental—postponed decisions, bad habits, excess "stuff," or maybe even laziness.

When you clean, you address dirt. When you organize you address behavior as well as the physical arrangement of items in a space. Organization is definitely the more important of the two. You can easily clean an organized space. You can also easily organize a dirty space. But cleaning a disorganized space is very difficult. It is hard to get at the dirt when everything is in utter chaos.

Once you have de-cluttered, focus on organizing and setting up systems to maintain the organization. Set up an incoming mail sorting system, a system to pay bills, a system to track projects and all assorted pieces.

> If you jump into organizing, you'll just be organizing stuff you won't keep. If you try to clean first, you'll spend a lot of energy cleaning things you will later remove.

Why do all these things first? Because your time is important and you'll spend far less time cleaning an organized space.

After you've de-cluttered, organized and begun deep cleaning, you'll want your house to stay that way. How? You put it on a schedule.

Did I mention a calendar as a housekeeping tool? It should be counted among the dust rags and cleansers—for it is just as important. We'll talk about a master calendar shortly, but for now know that figuring out a schedule for your housekeeping is critical. Some things are done daily—others weekly—others seasonally—a good schedule will help keep you from forgetting.

Does this sound dreadful? Think of this as a way to buy time when you need it. You won't ever have to waste a terrific fall Saturday on housework if you've done it in small pieces during the week.

Don't forget the "one more thing principle"

If there is only one principle to remember when considering house-work, it is the "One More Thing" principle. How many times do you rush off to another task before completing the task you're on? I know you remember to turn off the stove. But why not go ahead and put those last few dirty dishes in the dishwasher? Doing one more thing before you move on to the next task will ensure that when you return, things will be a little more in order. Continual employment of this principle will train you to do mini "pickups" all throughout your day, with the result being a home that doesn't get quite as out of hand as it could. Train your family members to do these things as well.

Often your one more thing will be to use one of the other principles you're learning, such as "Handle It Once" or "Determine a Place for Everything." Try it for a week. You'll be surprised how much time you eventually save when you spend a few minutes proactively dealing with chaos before it spirals out of control.

> Surrender the goal of perfection. Does Martha Stewart ever stop by your house? Probably not.

End the quest for perfection

I'm a recovering perfectionist. Perfectionism used to keep me worn out. Mop the kitchen floor? I'd do it until it was surgical-suite clean. It still got dirty in between and even though it was clean enough to eat off of, no one did so but the dog. But my perfectionism wouldn't let me simply do an adequate job and move on. I wasted a lot of time on my kitchen floor.

Have you ever decided to straighten up the house, only to wind up deep cleaning one room while the rest of the house remains in shambles? If it is spring-cleaning time for you, fine. But if you were just trying to tidy up on Sunday evening in order to get ready for the week, and you spent six hours cleaning the bathroom only to fall into bed before getting the laundry done, you'll wake up Monday with no clean clothes, despite the pristine bathroom.

Surrender the goal of perfection. Does Martha Stewart ever stop by your house? Probably not. So put away your visions of Martha Stewart-like perfection and settle for a household standard that leaves you time and energy for the things you find important—perhaps eating better, exercising more, or simply enjoying life.

> My home is not perfect. But it is peaceful enough that I enjoy being home. That'll do.

Our goal for housework is somewhere along the lines of "Clean enough that I enjoy living in my house," or the way I like to phrase it "Fifteen minutes from company." Am I ready for company at all times? No, but if someone dropped by, I could open the door and invite them in. But if they called and said, "I'm on my way," in 15 minutes I'd be ready for almost anyone, except perhaps Martha Stewart.

It is not perfect. But it is peaceful enough that I enjoy being home. That'll do.

Here's how I deal with a latent perfectionist tendency. I set a kitchen timer, and tell myself, "I'll spend five minutes on this shower enclosure. When the timer rings, I rinse and move on. Funny—five minutes of cleaning looks a lot like 20 minutes' worth.

Listen to the experts

Read *Speed Cleaning* by Jeff Campbell. This guy does housecleaning for a living, and he's made a science of doing it fast. He has tons of information about how to do the job and what type of cleaner or equipment to do it with. This book is perhaps my favorite house-work book. (It is also short and very entertaining—plus it presents a master plan on involving other family members in the cleaning process.)

Laundry

If you really don't like laundry, avoid it like the plague! Okay—I know you have to have nice clothes to wear to work and church—but try to think "laundry avoidance" whenever possible.

Play clothes are a lot easier to wash and fold than "dress" clothes. So teach your children to change their clothes before going outside to play. (Teach your husband the same thing!)

Remember our little pep talk about perfectionism? Think about lowering your standards when it comes to laundry. Make it a point to wear as many items as you can more than once between washings. (This is better for most clothes, too.) Unless your family is exceptionally dirty, you can probably go two weeks between bed linen changes instead of a week.

I know a member of my extended family whose family uses fresh towels every time they bathe or shower. I'm sure fresh towels are wonderfully fluffy, but what if she were to teach her family to hang their towels up to dry and re-used them for several days? If each towel were hung up and dried after each use and used for three days, she'd wash about 13 towels every week instead of 35. Think of the time (and energy and water and detergent) saved.

If you do laundry at home, pick your laundry days and stick to them. If something "misses" the hamper and doesn't get washed, too bad—it'll have to wait for the next laundry day. I use this simple rule and have determined that my laundry day is Sunday. So on Sundays when family obligations keep me busy visiting relatives and such, my husband knows that I won't have as much time to do laundry. If he accepts multiple commitments, I may not even get to the laundry. In that case, he waits (or does his own).

My record for not having a free Sunday was about four weeks. By the end of the four weeks we were wearing some interesting outfits—but amazingly we had enough clothes to go that long. We didn't die for lack of clean laundry. It may not have been our best fashion month, but we survived.

> Cleaner, sparer closets also mean that your fresh clothing won't be wrinkled before the next wearing.

Clean out your closets! Cleaner, sparer closets also mean that your fresh clothing won't be crammed and stuffed back in, only to get wrinkled before the next wearing. Have you ever had a shirt professionally laundered, and then found it got so wrinkled in your closet you had to iron it to make it presentable? That circumstance will cause a bad case of laundry blues.

20

Cooking

Let me describe to you, "Gretchen's I Hate Cooking Method of Dealing with Cooking and Groceries." First off, I have to be honest: my husband does the real cooking in my house. He starts with a roux. I start with a can of condensed mushroom soup. When he cooks, I usually clean. When I cook, I clean. I like cleaning a whole lot more than cooking!

Because I am not a "natural" in the kitchen, it is easy for me to procrastinate on the tasks that would make kitchen life easier. Here's a master plan we have developed that results in our having semi-nutritious meals four to six times a week.

Make a list of complete meals that you know how to cook and your family will eat. When you create your list, think of things that will generate leftovers that can be eaten at least one more time. Allow for dietary considerations. It is also a good idea to follow the general rule about having multiple colors of fruits and vegetables in each meal. You want to try and create meals as healthful as your family will eat.

I'd also consider the preparation and cleanup time. This isn't just a one-week list, this is a family master list. You don't have to use it forever, and you should probably reevaluate it a couple of times a year.

From your master menu, create a master grocery list. It sounds like a silly suggestion, but trust me, if you take this next step, even your teenage son will be able to do most of your grocery shopping.

You're going to index the grocery store. If your store provides a pretty detailed floor plan you might be able to skip this step, but if not, it is worth the time. Taking a clipboard, go up and down each grocery store aisle, one side at a time. You are looking for the name of every product your family uses on that aisle. If you don't use anchovy paste—don't write it down. But if your family uses ten other things nearby—write down all of them. I'd even indicate the brand, if you are selective. Do this up and down every aisle in the store. You now have a master grocery list of everything your family buys. If you want, type the list up. I just keep mine on large index cards, one per aisle, so I can flip through them easily.

Now that you've gotten this master list, cross-check it against your menus. This step is the time to make sure when you shop you get every single item to create everything on your menus. No more half-made meatloaf only to go to the pantry to find no tomato paste.

Mark the items needed for your menus as "must have on hand items." You'll also want to mark other household essentials—bathroom tissue, soap and such. The idea is, if you always have these things in your freezer and pantry, you always have a meal ready to go.

> Because I am not a "natural" in the kitchen, it is easy for me to procrastinate on the tasks that would make kitchen life easier.

Each week when you make up your grocery list, use this master list to create your weekly shopping list. In our house it is not uncommon for my husband to have his head in the pantry, with me calling out items while he yells back, "Green beans? Three cans!"

Things we need, I add to my list. When I am finished, I have a list of products to buy and it is in order that items are arranged in the grocery store.

This method doesn't solve the issue of having to actually cook the meals, but I have found the fewer decisions there are to make, and the more accessible the ingredients, the less of a chore cooking really is. And since I have created menus that generate leftovers, I try to have a "heat up" night in between every "cook" night.

It is also good to periodically declare war on stored food, both canned and frozen, to clean out your inventory. You don't want to stumble over cream corn from two years ago.

Make it a point to cook one bulk meal at least one day a week. By this I mean something that is just as easy to cook 20 servings as two. Chili and soup are good examples. So are casseroles to freeze. If you are making one batch of wild rice casserole, doubling the recipe is not much extra trouble at all.

Give yourself a break, too. If it works in your budget, go out to eat one night each week—or declare Sunday as "pizza" or "leftover" night and spend the time you would have spent cooking watching a family movie or playing a game.

21

How to Organize an Event

Organizing an event is a terrifying experience for some people. While it can be tedious, making an event happen—from a small seminar to a lavish event for 2,200 is just a matter of organizing the task.

Develop a mission statement.

Start any event planning with a mission statement. This first step is very important. If you ever read the "Dear Abby" column in the paper, at least several times a year a distressed bride (or mother of the bride) writes in begging for help in planning an event that is wrought with emotion. Usually the problem has to do with varying ideas of what a wedding should be like.

That's a mission statement problem. If all the parties involved sat down and honestly expressed their expectations on the front end, negotiated in a level-headed manner, and then crafted a mission statement, the planning and production of the wedding would be much easier.

How do you create a mission statement for an event?

To craft an event mission statement, begin with the end product in mind. What do you want the event to be like? (You can ignore money for a minute while we hash out the details.) Is intimate and cozy more important than big and splashy? If you take anywhere from ten minutes to an hour to really think about what you want out of your event, you'll be in a good position to write a three or four sentence mission statement. Include others involved, if necessary. Create a picture of your "ideal" event. List the elements you feel are critical to the event's success.

Write this statement down. A written mission statement is a real mission statement. One you carry in your head is just the glimmer of an idea.

Now we analyze the mission statement. Is it realistic? If your budget is lemonade, don't plan for champagne. If champagne is the most important thing, then be ready to make cuts in other areas.

What are the other problems you see with your event? With the help of others involved, create a master list of "issues" that are in the way of your event. This stage is where you brainstorm and try to find out the weak point of your plan. Go ahead and write these down, as it is good to be mindful of them.

> To craft an event mission statement, begin with the end product in mind. What do you want the event to be like?

Now, with your list of potential problems, go back and adjust your mission statement accordingly. If space is an issue, reduce the size of the event, or find a bigger venue. If money is an issue, focus on the things that really matter and eliminate things that matter less. With this revised mission statement, you are ready to begin planning a detailed list of everything you need to do.

With your mission statement in front of you, make a list of everything that has to happen for the event to be created in accordance with your mission. This can be a stream of consciousness exercise. Try using 3x5 cards for this, since they can be shuffled. Put down all your wishes, hopes and dreams, too. We know that some aren't possible, but go ahead and put them down. This task may take several sessions, but try to make as comprehensive a list as you can, as it will be used to create your master plan.

Once you have all your "things that have to happen" in front of you, you probably see how overwhelming the task is. This is where we become very realistic. Delete everything from your "has to happen" list that can possibly be deleted! About those "wishes" and "dreams" that were written down, pay attention to these and try to honor the ones that can be honored. For those that are simply not going to happen, it is better to write down the dream, and consciously delete it than to have a glimmer of hope for it in the back of your mind, secretly complicating every decision.

From your remaining items, develop a time line. Make it as detailed as possible and start as far out from the event as is realistic. Now that we've gotten the time line, it may be that you see there is more than can be comfortably handled within the parameters you are operating. Once again, delete things that are unnecessary. (Now that you see how much there is to do, your standards may drop.)

Sit down with your time line and your personal calendar and write everything on your time line in the calendar. Take special notice of time crunches. You'll need to get help with these areas. You'll probably need to put a comprehensive time line in the back of your calendar to consult from time to time when you need to review the big picture in addition to the tasks on your daily reminder list.

Next, look over the entries in your calendar and mark those that need advance notice to address. Flip a few days forward and give yourself advance notice. Now you have a master plan and calendar for your event. All you have to do is to get started.

> **Develop a time line. Make it as detailed as possible and start as far out from the event as is realistic.**

One way to get started is to figure out your least enjoyable task—and do it or delegate it, in order to break the blockage that stops you from starting the project.

As you complete your event planning and production, be sure to keep notes of what worked—especially for events, and review these notes before you begin your next project.

Planning an event: Thanksgiving Dinner

An event that nearly all of us have at some point in our lives is Thanksgiving. I have jotted down below my thoughts on getting ready for this event. My event will be small, not more than 20 people. Thus, the preparations are rather simple. This method can be used for a more complex event, too.

First, what has to happen between now and Thanksgiving morning? I try to think of everything I want done. (Some may get eliminated—like edging the sidewalk—but it is good to at least think about it, just in case time presents itself.)

Event:	Deadline:
Set Guest List	_____
Invite & confirm guests	_____
Set menu	_____
Shop	_____
Edge sidewalk	_____
Rake leaves	_____
Clean gutters (if time)	_____
Vacuum house	_____
Set table	_____
Set up folding table	_____
Tablecloths	_____
Centerpiece, etc.	_____
Napkins ironed and folded	_____
Cook ahead anything possible:	
Dessert	_____
Tea	_____
Other	_____
Other	_____
Make appetizer & punch	_____
Thaw turkey	_____
Prep turkey in browning bag night before	_____

Below there is a time line for the day of the event. I make one of these up for almost any event, from a professional conference to a casual party. A time line has several benefits.

One major advantage in writing down everything is that it shows you when you will have a time crunch. In the case of Thanksgiving, I know right off the bat that I need to use ready-made rolls. I have only one oven, so I need to plan for what hours the oven will be at what temperature. Desserts can be made the day before, which will relieve the burden on my single oven.

This time line also tells me when I need to delegate, and when I need to simplify. All of these things become apparent when you establish a time frame.

Time Line, Day of Event: Thanksgiving

8:15	Turkey in oven (Gretchen)
8:30	Make dressing (Gretchen)
9:00	Set up coffee maker (Gretchen)
9:30	Prepare vegetables for steaming (Bill)
9:40	Prepare vegetables for stove top (Gretchen)
10:00	Get out plates and glasses (Gretchen)
10:30	Put sweet potatoes in oven (Bill)
11:00	Put out appetizer & punch (Gretchen)
11:15	Turkey out of oven (Bill)
11:15	Put dressing in oven (Gretchen)
11:30	Make gravy (Bill)
11:30	Turn on vegetable steamer (Gretchen)
11:30	Start stove top vegetables (Gretchen)
11:45	Slice turkey (Bill)
11:45	Rolls in oven (Gretchen)
11:50	Ice in glasses (Gretchen or guest)
11:50	Sweet potatoes out of oven (Bill)
11:50	Set up buffet line:
	Turkey
	Sweet potatoes
	Misc. vegetables
	Dressing
	Gravy
	Tea and water
11:55	Blessing (Bill)
12:00	Begin buffet line (Everybody)
12:00	Turn on coffee maker (Gretchen)
12:05	Pass rolls (Gretchen)
1:00	Announce dessert (Self-serve)

Having lists like this posted in your kitchen will help you delegate to "helpful" guests who insist on doing something, even when you've got it under control. For larger events—say more than 25 people, the time line works the same way, but you simplify as much as possible. The largest sit-down dinner party I've ever hosted in my home had 36 guests. The menu was excruciatingly simple: pork roast, lima beans, citrus wild rice and rolls. Dessert was already on the tables, as were pitchers of tea, water and carafes of hot coffee. It was served buffet style. I was able to enjoy it, too.

22

The Ultimate To Do List: Your Master List

We've talked about your calendar and how important it is, but to maximize its use, you'll want a "Master List" to go along with it. What is a Master List? It is your most comprehensive list possible of all the things you and your family must attend to each year.

This wonderful list will include all your regular health appointments—from orthodontist visits to annual physicals. It will include your pet's vet check, too. You will put on this calendar everything you do seasonally—from pressure washing the deck in the spring to putting up storm windows in the fall. You won't put on it carpool duty, or weekly swimming lessons—these go in your calendar. You should, however, note the beginning and ending of swim season.

How to create a master list
Begin with ample blank paper. Label different sheets of paper with appropriate headings, such as Home Maintenance, Health, Christmas, Vacation, plus any categories you need for work projects that occur annually. You'll want to be sure to include anything that is a big commitment—from Church to Scouts—as well as little seasonal things that are important to a well-run house. I'd even include car oil changes and filter changes for your air conditioner and furnace.

Jot on each appropriate list everything you can think of that falls in that category. As you write, you'll think up whole new categories to add—just pull out a separate piece of paper. You may want to give yourself two or three sessions of brainstorming for this job. It is very much like planning an event—and you are! You are planning a year in your family's life.

Once you've added everything you need to do in your life, you'll need to divide the tasks up by months. Most calendars are too small, so start with 12 sheets of notebook paper labeled for the months of the year and start with your first list and assign every task to a month.

> Creating a family master list is very much like planning an event—and you are! You are planning a year in your family's life.

Some tasks "belong" in certain months, but other things are more flexible. You might want to save the flexible tasks for last and see what months are the least busy and put those events in the less frantic months.

Now, once you've taken all your lists and divided them up into 12 months of tasks—get out a calendar. You'll need to write all your tasks down on a family master calendar. Many of the tasks will need to go on your personal calendar, too.

Keep your 12 monthly pages and don't throw away the pages of your family master calendar as the year goes by—instead keep both sets to use to create next year's master calendar.

When you do this, it will be instantly obvious if a new plan interferes with something scheduled on your master calendar. If your family vacation is in June, but that's also an opportunity for your son to go to summer camp, as soon as you flip to the page you'll see the potential conflict. Your calendar isn't set in stone and you can modify things. But keeping the master calendar in combination with your master to do list will help you avoid double-booking big commitments.

23

Managing Your Priorities

A priority is merely a ranking you give to an item, giving it weight in the quest for your time and attention. The things you give attention to are your priorities, whether by your own conscious choice or by default from lack of planning. Here are some guidelines for managing your priorities.

Admit you can't do everything

In a perfect world, there is adequate time for all the tasks you face each day. If you had adequate time, setting priorities would only be a matter of doing the items due first before addressing the items due later. But this is not a perfect world, even though some people prioritize only by "due date." By admitting that accomplishing everything is not only unlikely, but also perhaps impossible, you then become ready to actually make meaningful decisions about your priorities. As long as you keep telling yourself "I can do all of this if I work hard enough" you will have difficulty prioritizing. You may also drive yourself insane.

> As long as you keep telling yourself "I can do all of this if I work hard enough" you will have difficulty prioritizing.

"Management" comes first

Management issues usually cause more headache than other types of issues. What's a "management issue?" An example might be best to illustrate. For those of you ever involved in a personnel dispute, you understand the impact of a management issue on your productivity.

One dysfunctional employee can demoralize a whole department. That's a management issue. If a large problem takes your time and energy away from your primary objective, make sure that problem is solved as quickly as possible. It is better to spend the energy to deal with the problem than to continue to let it drain you and the energy from an entire operation.

> If a large problem looms, taking your time and energy away from your primary objective, make sure that problem is solved as quickly as possible.

Address your fears

Sometimes when a task is daunting, we procrastinate. Admit your fear, and then use procrastination-breaking behaviors to get going on the project. Break it into small pieces or steps, set outside accountability...whatever it takes to get moving on a task. In most cases dreading a task is worse than doing a task.

If in doubt, throw it out

That could be the motto for this book, couldn't it? By it I mean, look at your To-Do list and decide to go ahead and delete those items that have been hanging around for months on end. It is better to admit you're never going to get the dog's teeth cleaned and drop it from the list rather than sighing over it every week.

If it is something that really can't be ignored—such as getting a new car inspection sticker—just do it. You can throw it off the list by simply doing it. But don't let an endless stream of inconsequential items clog your weekly planning. Get them done or give up on them.

Think geographically

Sometimes your daily priorities will fall out around errands or some specific type of activity (such as a morning scheduled to be spent doing correspondence on the computer). Group similar activities together. If you're going to be on the computer for three hours anyway, go ahead and type up the minutes for that meeting, too.

If you are out on errands, think about your total route and how many places you can cover in a single trip. You may be able to clump trips together and take care of multiple items on your list. Think creatively, too. If you only need one grocery item, consider going to the smaller store next to the hardware store. It may be a little more expensive at the smaller store, but when you factor in the convenience, it is probably cheaper in energy and time.

With seemingly equally important items, try thinking negatively

The question to ask here is "What is the greatest negative consequence of my not getting this done on time [or now]?" When two items appear equally important, this question can help you figure out which one comes with the greatest penalties for non-action.

Also factor in here non-tangible aspects of postponing something. If you put off re-working your closet and it aggravates you every morning, that daily hassle may add up to big negative impact in terms of the quality of your life. Who wants to be aggravated every morning?

If you hate being out of shape, but can't seem to make exercise a priority, factor in all the daily self-criticism you face and its impact on how you feel about yourself. Stopping daily self-loathing might be a higher priority than "getting fit."

Decide to do it

If an item is a high priority, and you know it, just do it. Sometimes it is easy to get sidetracked onto activities we enjoy more, but discipline can help us stay focused.

And it goes without saying:

■ Do the most important things first. (These are the things most central to your mission.)

■ Start the tasks that involve the most other people first, because committees take longer. And even as your start these "multiple people" tasks first, it is wise to allow for more time to get the tasks accomplished than you would if it were a solo assignment.

■ Delegate with clear guidelines and due dates. If your assignment doesn't have clear action dates, it will get pushed to the bottom of your delegatee's priority list.

■ Achieve balance between your priorities. Don't let a single task paralyze your work on other tasks. If you've come to a work stoppage—for whatever reason—park the blocked task and begin work on another task while you wait for the work stoppage to end.

24

Discipline: Getting What You Want

Organization requires action on our part. We have to do something. Even executives that can afford to hire (or can't afford not to hire) experts to help them become organized are left with required action. They have to keep themselves organized.

This point is where things can fall apart. It is one thing to experience the rush of energy that results from a newly organized workspace. But it is another thing entirely to dedicate a small portion of every jam-packed day to organization tasks, such as filing, sorting and tossing junk mail and using your calendar correctly instead of leaving appointments written on sticky notes.

The missing ingredient is discipline. We have to discipline ourselves to continue to do the small things that make us more organized. And it is self-discipline we are really talking about. Everyone has access to the same amount of self-discipline or self-control. 100%.

When we choose to put things away, write in our calendars, or toss junk mail we are making a deliberate choice. Consistently making the right choices results in a more organized life. Not all choices have to be perfect, of course. But the more right choices we make—to "do it now" rather than later, or to decide to throw it out, rather than stack it up for future consideration—the more we will find ourselves organized and enjoying the peace that comes from living a more organized life.

Discipline sounds like a very negative word. We associate it with punishment, reprimands, and compliance to rules we didn't make and don't like. But the type of discipline we want here is not negative. Discipline in this area is simply a matter of getting what we want.

Do you want an orderly workspace in your office or kitchen? If you really want it, then a series of small actions that you choose to make daily will give you what you want. That's discipline. No one has beaten you with a stick to make you act in a certain way. You have decided that an orderly workspace is worth your time and effort.

By consciously deciding what you want in your life, you can then determine what steps are needed to get it. Taking the steps to get there is discipline. Getting what you want is the end result.

And getting what you want out of life is truly a great thing.

Appendix A

Homework

If you really want meaningful change, you'll have to devote time to practice. This practice is called homework, and ideally you should set aside two to fours hours for it every week as you work to get your life organized.

Plan to return to this exercise weekly and continue to work at areas in your life that are really an annoyance. This exercise will lead you through an evaluation and help you set priorities for the areas which cause you the greatest angst. Start with the areas that bother you the most, in small, concrete pieces.

1. Evaluate your situation. Spend 30 minutes going around your home (or office — whichever is your primary focus) with a note pad. Open every cupboard, closet, drawer, etc. Take notes of what bugs you. Which room is the worst? Using this information, make an action plan, #2 below.

2. Set goals for organizing areas that bother you, listing your top five priorities. For your top five priorities, determine what needs to be done. Your list might look like this:

■ Living room. Hang picture over mantle, clear up magazines and papers. Find a place for the extra coffee table (Goodwill?) Rearrange accessories to a better configuration (eliminate some?)

■ Office. Figure out a filing system. File those papers on top of the filing cabinet. Set up a folder or some system to pay bills regularly.

■ Storage room. Clear out all junk and haul it away.

■ Kitchen. Organize the drawers and figure out where the stuff should go. Do SOMETHING (anything) with the pantry.

■ Master Closet. Try to set it up so I can find something to wear without trying on six outfits every morning.

3. Identify your top priority for organization. Number the items you identified, from most critical to least critical. All of these areas need attention, so they will be tackled sooner or later. You just want to create some overall plan of action.

Select your first priority. Decide whether this task can be tackled in one step or several. If it is a multi-step project, divide it into manageable portions.

For example, if your goal is to get your bedroom organized so it is a relaxing, not taxing, place, you might want to begin by organizing all visible horizontal surfaces, (i.e., dresser tops, night stands, etc).

4. Take action. Using the "Clutter Removal" method described on page 23, eliminate all excess items in this area and rearrange the remaining items in a manner that is pleasing to you.

Some Contemplation Questions:
As you completed this activity, think about your reactions to the elimination process. Was it difficult? Easy? Did you find yourself becoming motivated to do more, or less?
■ What was hardest?
■ Did you set priorities for areas to be addressed?
■ In looking at your list of what bugs you the most, was there a pattern from room to room or area to area? What kind of thing disturbs you the most?
■ Thinking about your de-cluttering action,
■ How did it go?
■ Was it hard to let go of some things?
■ Was it a relief to let go of some things?
■ Timing: What worked best for you: small blocks or large blocks of time?

Appendix B

Goal-Setting Exercise

An unrecorded goal is merely a wish. A documented goal is an action plan. If you will take some time to work through the exercises on the next six pages, you will be surprised at the result. There is something powerful about taking the time to consider and write out goals. When you couple your written goals with action steps—as indicated in the exercises that follow, your goals are even more powerful. For maximum results, once you've completed the goal-setting process, take out your personal calendar and record your intermediate steps as deadlines. Now you've got a master plan.

Goal Worksheet

Brainstorm: The chaotic or disorganized areas that I need to work on most are: (list in any order)

Of the above areas, circle three to four that are the biggest for you.

To determine how big the issue is, ask yourself this question in each area: "What are the negative consequences I face if I do not improve in this area?" The areas with the greatest negative consequences should be circled. Don't forget to calculate non-tangible consequences—such as daily aggravation. Now, again thinking in terms of the consequences or personal costs involved, rate the circled areas from One (Most Important) to Four (Of Lesser Importance).

1._____

2._____

3._____

4._____

For each of the areas listed above, use the following pages to develop a GOAL for improvement and ACTION Plan to address the area. Start by transferring the item on each line above to its corresponding goal sheet. Reword the item into a goal.

Goal #1

My goal is:

My deadline for accomplishment is:

Here are the steps I can take to meet this goal:

Time Frame   **Action or Step**

_____ _____

_____ _____

_____ _____

_____ _____

_____ _____

_____ _____

_____ _____

_____ _____

A reward I can give myself for accomplishing this goal is:

Goal #2

My goal is:

My deadline for accomplishment is:

Here are the steps I can take to meet this goal:

Time Frame   **Action or Step**

_____   _____

_____   _____

_____   _____

_____   _____

_____   _____

_____   _____

_____   _____

_____   _____

A reward I can give myself for accomplishing this goal is:

Goal #3

My goal is:

My deadline for accomplishment is:

Here are the steps I can take to meet this goal:

Time Frame	Action or Step
_____	_____
_____	_____
_____	_____
_____	_____
_____	_____
_____	_____
_____	_____

A reward I can give myself for accomplishing this goal is:

Goal #4

My goal is:

My deadline for accomplishment is:

Here are the steps I can take to meet this goal:

Time Frame	Action or Step
_____	_____
_____	_____
_____	_____
_____	_____
_____	_____
_____	_____
_____	_____
_____	_____

A reward I can give myself for accomplishing this goal is:

About the Author

Gretchen Cook is a library director, writer and magazine editor. Staying focused on the desired outcome, staying organized and working—step-by-step—toward her goal is the way she lives. Whether she's hosting a couple of friends at a dinner party or a couple of thousand high school students at a college fair, she's found organization is a critical element in getting things done with as little stress as possible.

Gretchen Cook holds a bachelor's and a master's degrees from Florida State University. She has been an academic library director for 15 years. In 1998, realizing that library science was essentially a degree in organization, she began teaching classes on personal organization.

The book you hold is the result of classroom discussions with her many students. In addition to being a library director, Gretchen Cook is a freelance writer, magazine editor and publisher of *Parents & Kids Magazine, Gulf Coast Parents & Kids Magazine,* the *Parents & Kids Academic Year Family Planner* and the *Parents & Kids College Planner.*

Gretchen Cook has presented her lectures all over the Eastern United States to groups as varied as church organizations, professional chefs, college presidents and civic groups. If your group or professional organization could benefit from an entertaining and energizing class on organization, please contact her at 601-366-0901.

She lives in Jackson, Mississippi.

Give *Organize Your Life: Skills you need to conquer the areas of chaos in your life* to your friends and colleagues. Check your local bookstore, or order with this form.

____Yes, I want _____ copies of *Organize Your Life* for $14.95.
____Yes, I am interested in having Gretchen Cook give a seminar on personal organization. Please send me more information.

> For book orders please note the following discount schedule:
> 1 copy – no discount
> 2-4 copies – 20% discount
> 5-99 copies – 40% discount
> 100 + copies – 50% discount

Include $3.95 shipping and handling for the first book and $1.50 for each additional book ordered. Mississippi residents, please add 7% sales tax to order total (including and handling). Payment must accompany orders.

My check or money order for $_____is enclosed. Make your check payable and return to Bella Luna Productions, PO Box 4406, Jackson, MS 39216.

Name:_____

Organization:_____

Address:_____

City/State/Zip:_____

Phone:_____ Email:_____
For MasterCard, VISA or Discover:

Credit Card #_____

3 digit code on back of card:_____ Expiration date:_____

Daytime phone number:_____

Signature:_____
Call 1-877-466-7927   Fax: 601-366-0966